ISLAM, ISRAEL AND THE WEST

Also by
Danny Burmawi

The God of my Grandmother
Questions Christians Should
Ask Muslims

ISLAM, ISRAEL AND THE WEST

A FORMER MUSLIM'S ANALYSIS

DANNY BURMAWI

GERASA

Islam, Israel and the West.

Copyright © 2025 by Danny Burmawi. All rights reserved. Printed in the United States of America. No part of this book may be used or reproduced in any manner whatsoever without written permission except in the case of brief quotations embodied in critical articles and reviews.

FIRST EDITION

Library of Congress Cataloging-in-Publication Data
Names: Burmawi, Danny, 1988– author.
Title: Islam, Israel and the West / A Former Muslim's Analysis, Danny Burmawi.

Identifiers: LCCN 2025920138
ISBN 979-8-9930154-9-1 | ISBN 979-8-9930154-8-4 (ebook)

Subjects: LCSH: Arab-Israeli |Middle East | Islam, Christianity

ISBN 979-8-9930154-9-1

For my ancestors —
I have broken the chains that were forced upon you.
Your silence is no longer my inheritance.

CONTENTS

Introduction	ix
1. What is Islam?	1
2. The Islamic War on Israel	29
3. Why Islam is Incompatible with the West	71
4. Rebranding Islam	107
5. The Foreign God	145
6. The New Frontiers	177
Notes	215
About the Author	227

INTRODUCTION

On October 9, 2023 — just two days after Hamas's massacre in Israel[1] —I sat on a bench in Chicago's Millennium Park, speaking Arabic on the phone with a friend. My wife and child were beside me. A woman with her children sat down nearby, but the instant she heard my voice, she pulled her kids close and fled. I barely noticed until my wife leaned over and whispered, "She was wearing a Star of David."

While Jewish families in Israel were still identifying bodies—while the wounds of the October 7 massacre were still raw—the streets of Western cities were already erupting in protest. Palestinian flags waved in New York, London, and Sydney. Chants of "intifada" and calls to erase Israel from the map echoed through public squares, even before Israel had launched any retaliation. In Chicago, just two months later, on New Year's Eve, I walked down Michigan Avenue and saw nearly fifteen thousand people marching[2]—a chaotic coalition of feminists, LGBT activists, BLM supporters, Jewish youth in keffiyehs, Christians in clerical collars, and African Americans—all led by Muslim immigrants.

I approached a white woman holding a sign that read, *"From the river to the sea, Palestine will be free."* I asked, "Do you know what that means?" Her eyes narrowed. "You think you're standing against genocide," I said, "but you're calling for one." She didn't answer. She screamed over me instead. Within seconds, a group of twenty to thirty people surrounded me—their faces twisted in rage, their bodies pressing in. My wife clutched our baby. Instinctively, I scanned the crowd, calculating how to get them to safety. Police intervened and escorted us away.

For fifteen years I had been running—driven from my country because of my faith, forced to hide my political beliefs, and ultimately leaving the Middle East because I wanted my son to grow up in a place where we would not have to flee for who we are. I came to America believing the running was over. Yet there I was, in the heart of Chicago, watching a Jewish woman flee for who she was, and moments later fleeing myself, with my wife and child, for what we stood for. The fear that shaped the Middle East had crossed the ocean. The world I thought I left behind had arrived ahead of me.

For the past two years, this scene has played out across the globe. From New York to London, Toronto to Berlin, public spaces have been taken over by waves of demonstrators with Palestinian flags, accusing Israel of genocide. University campuses have become flashpoints—lawns turned into encampments, buildings seized, graduation ceremonies disrupted.[3] In multiple cities, protests have turned violent. In Southern California, Paul Kessler, a sixty-nine-year-old Jewish man, died after being struck in the head with a megaphone during a protest confrontation.[4] In Washington, D.C., a young Israeli-American couple—Yaron Lischinsky and Sarah Milgrim, both staffers at the Israeli Embassy—were gunned down outside the Capital Jewish Museum as they left a diplomatic event.[5] In France and Germany, Jewish businesses and synagogues came under attack. In Australia and the UK, crowds openly chanted "Gas the Jews." Thousands of Jews and their allies have been harassed, assaulted, and threatened —for expressing support for Israel or simply for being visibly Jewish. Students have been spat on, doxxed, shoved, and stalked. Some were advised by university staff to stay home or remove their kippahs for safety.[6]

Why does a territorial dispute involving one of the smallest countries on earth—a nation no larger than New Jersey—continue to dominate the global conversation more than seventy-five years after its birth? Why is the Arab-Israeli conflict, above all others, the one that fills the streets with protesters, hijacks campuses, ignites parliaments, floods headlines, and dictates the tone of international diplomacy? It is not the bloodiest conflict of our time. The Syrian civil war has claimed more than half a million lives[7], yet it barely registers in Western discourse. It is not the most complex. The crisis in Kashmir—an active flashpoint between two nuclear powers—elicits global indifference. It is not the most recent, nor the most destabilizing. Yemen remains in the grip of a devastating famine and civil war, with tens of thousands of children dying of malnutrition.[8] Libya is a failed state fractured by tribal conflict and foreign intervention, its people trafficked and its society shattered. Sudan is being torn apart by a brutal internal war that has displaced millions and triggered famine. In Nigeria, Christians are being slaughtered in numbers that rival modern genocides[9], yet no Western government calls it a "moral emergency." But when it comes to Israel, everything changes. Every inch of land, every missile, every casualty, every policy decision—no matter how defensive or justified—is magnified, condemned, and politicized.

In recent decades, the Palestinian cause has been embraced with fervor by Western political, academic, and social spheres. Student unions across North America and Europe have made Palestinian advocacy a cornerstone of their activism, organizing protests, divestment campaigns, and resolutions that frame the cause as a stand against oppression.[10] Academic institutions, particularly in the humanities and social sciences, have woven Palestinian narratives into their curricula, using the conflict to critique Western foreign policy and postcolonial legacies. Human rights NGOs and media outlets amplify these narratives through reports, documentaries, and editorials, constantly emphasizing Palestinian suffering and Israeli aggression. Political figures and United Nations bodies further elevate the cause, embedding it within international human rights frameworks. In progressive circles, supporting Palestine is no longer just a position, it's a badge of moral superiority, a way to signal commitment to social justice, anti-imperialism, and equity. Its symbolic power galvanizes diverse groups, from grassroots activists to policymakers, under a shared banner of resistance.

This Western obsession mirrors the Palestinian cause's historical role in Arab and Islamic discourse. Since 1948, the cause has been a central pillar of political rhetoric across the Middle East. Leaders like Gamal Abdel Nasser, King Faisal of Saudi Arabia, Saddam Hussein, Hafiz al-Assad, and Muammar Gaddafi, alongside groups like the Muslim Brotherhood, the Ayatollah regime in Iran, Hezbollah, and the Houthis, all of them have consistently raised the Palestinian banner. It has been central to every major summit, speech, and United Nations address, serving as the emotional core of Arab nationalism and a unifying cry for regimes otherwise divided by ideology, religion, or geopolitics. No other issue has commanded such sustained rhetorical devotion, dominating Arab media, diplomacy, and discourse across decades. The cause transcended divides and united monarchs and revolutionaries, Sunnis and Shiites, secularists and religious factions in a way no other cause has achieved.

What's striking is that while the Palestinian cause has been central to both the Arab and Islamic worlds, the Palestinian people themselves never were. Growing up in Jordan, I lived just minutes away from Palestinian refugee camps—Gaza Camp in Jerash and Prince Hassan Camp in Amman. What I saw with my own eyes stood in grotesque contrast to how the Palestinian cause was championed by our leaders and institutions. I saw crumbling infrastructure, families crammed into tiny rooms, and children playing in streets strewn with debris. This paradox was not unique to Jordan; it spanned the entire Arab world. In Lebanon, as of 2023, nearly 489,000 registered Palestinian refugees are barred from owning property, denied work permits, excluded from unions, and cut off from state healthcare, trapped in 12 overcrowded camps marked by poverty and decay.[11] In Syria, before and during the civil war, some 560,000 Palestinians lived under constant surveillance and discrimination, with camps like Yarmouk bombed into ruins.[12] In Egypt and Iraq, integration has been deliberately avoided, keeping Palestinian communities in a state of permanent limbo.[13]

This contrast makes clear that the Palestinian cause, kept alive for more than seventy-seven years, was never truly about the rights of the Palestinian people. Something else sustained it in the Arab and Islamic world. To uncover what that something was—and how it explains the West's fixation on the Palestinian cause—we must go back to the streets of Amman in 2006. That year, Israel launched Operation Summer Rains in Gaza in response to the kidnapping of soldier Gilad Shalit by Hamas.[14] I was sixteen years old, marching through my city alongside Jordanians and Palestinians. We shouted anti-Israel slogans and burned Israeli flags. None of it was unusual; this reaction was expected whenever Israel responded militarily. The incursion into Gaza, intended to stop rocket fire and recover a captured soldier, was instantly branded an act of aggression, and outrage spread across the Arab and Islamic world.

But like many Jordanians, I felt no bond with the Palestinian people. From a young age, I had been taught to see them not as neighbors but as a destabilizing force within our country. My grandmother often spoke to me about

Black September in the 1970s, when Palestinian militias seized control of parts of Jordan and turned their weapons on Jordanians.[15] One memory she passed down was about my uncle, an eleven-year-old orphan at the time, harassed by armed Palestinians while trying to earn money to feed his younger siblings. For us, Palestinians were remembered as the source of internal chaos that nearly pushed Jordan to collapse.

And yet, I marched. I didn't protest because I cared about Palestinian rights. I protested because I was a Muslim.

While the Palestinian cause is presented on the global stage as a political struggle—a fight over land, sovereignty, and resistance to occupation—in the Islamic world that was never what sent people into the streets. For us, it was not political. It was theological. Just months before the 2006 Gaza conflict, my devotion to Islam had deepened profoundly, sparked by the Danish cartoon controversy of late 2005. The publication of cartoons depicting the Prophet Muhammad in *Jyllands-Posten* sent shockwaves of rage across the Islamic world.[16] I was particularly moved by a sermon from Kuwaiti Imam Khalid al-Rashid titled *"Oh Ummah of Muhammad."*[17] He spoke about how the Prophet's companions defended him against any insult, recounting stories of their extreme loyalty: killing poets who criticized Muhammad and bringing their heads to him, even one companion beheading his own father for refusing to accept Islam.[18] Al-Rashid described the worship-like devotion every Muslim should have for the Prophet—citing how companions fought over his spittle to receive blessings, how a woman was praised for drinking his urine, and how the Quran glorifies those who defend the Prophet's honor without hesitation. He warned that the Prophet's enemies still exist today, that Islam remains under attack, and that the West conspires day and night to weaken the ummah*—with Israel as the front line of this global conspiracy.

That is why I was marching in the streets against Israel that day. That is why we celebrated every time a Palestinian stabbed an Israeli, every time a suicide bomber killed dozens of Jews. We did not care who the victims were, and we certainly did not care about the land. In truth, most of us could not have cared less about it. If given the chance, millions of Arabs would abandon it in a heartbeat—just look at how they risk their lives crossing the Mediterranean in plastic boats, forsaking their so-called "beloved" lands for the mere hope of stepping onto the shores of Europe.

There is no way to separate Islam from the Arab-Israeli conflict. The struggle is steeped in Islamic theology, history, and doctrine. From the chant of "Khaybar, Khaybar"[19] to the lessons in schoolbooks, sermons from mosque pulpits, and the narratives in media, the rhetoric is overtly religious. Israel is not perceived as a colonial project but as a theological threat. Jews are portrayed as infidels who rejected Muhammad, and as the front line of the West's ongoing conspiracy against Islam.

In the mind of every Muslim—no matter how moderate

---

* **Ummah:** an Arabic term meaning "community" or "nation." In Islamic usage, it refers specifically to the global community of Muslims, united by religion rather than geography or nationality.

or secular they appear—the conflict with Israel is, at its core, a religious war. For Muslims worldwide, Palestine is not a Palestinian issue; it is an Islamic one. This is why leaders who bypass the cause and pursue peace with Israel are branded traitors to the faith, declared apostates, and, when possible, assassinated.[20]

The hostility toward Jews did not begin with the modern conflict or with the establishment of Israel. Long before any occupation, Islamic attitudes toward Jews were embedded in the Qur'an and the sayings of Muhammad, as we will see. This is what makes the conflict both personal and compulsory. It would not be an exaggeration to say that, in the collective subconscious of the Islamic world, standing against Israel ranks among the highest religious obligations.

Islam is a total system of laws and expectations so expansive and demanding that failure is inevitable. Guilt becomes constant. But Islam offers a way to offset that failure: pledge allegiance to the faith, stand with the ummah, and oppose its enemies. And nothing signals that allegiance more loudly than standing against Israel. In a world of impossible demands, this becomes the simplest, most accessible proof of loyalty.

This is why the Arab-Israeli narrative in the Islamic world is uncompromising—devoid of nuance and leaving no space for alternative perspectives. Israel is not merely opposed; it is demonized, portrayed as the embodiment of evil, with Jews—and, behind them, the West—cast as the enemies of Allah. In this worldview, enemies plot, conspire, and seek to annihilate both you and your faith. Whether you are a villager in Yemen or a professor at

Harvard, if Islam frames your outlook, self-reflection on this point becomes impossible. To entertain doubt or consider Israel's side would fracture the foundation of your worldview, threatening the soteriological comfort that comes from participating in a divine struggle.

Spiritual security, in this mindset, depends on unwavering opposition to Allah's foes. Any revision, any hesitation, even the slightest crack through which questioning or doubt may enter, risks unraveling the certainty that shields the believer from guilt and divine retribution. As we will explore in later chapters, this rigid narrative—rooted in Islamic theology—ensures that the Palestinian cause endures as a monolithic rallying cry for a cosmic battle against a demonized enemy, closing off the possibility of dialogue or introspection.

Just as the Palestinian cause in the Arab world serves as a shell for religious hatred, in the West it functions as a shell for something else. The twentieth century unleashed a wave of ideological revolutions—Marxism, postmodernism, and critical theory—that reshaped Western thought. Marxism reframed history as a struggle between oppressors and oppressed. Critical theory cast every social structure, law, tradition, and belief as an instrument of domination. These currents converged into a radical leftist worldview that saw Western civilization—its capitalism, traditions, colonial past, and moral framework—as inherently oppressive.

Within this framework, non-Western societies were

reimagined as victims and the West as the permanent aggressor. The Palestinian cause became the quintessential struggle of the oppressed against the oppressor, with Israel—and by extension the West—portrayed as the colonial villain.[21] Leftist academics, activists, and students embraced this manufactured narrative, seeing in Palestine a powerful weapon to critique Western power structures.

Islam, in turn, leveraged this to amplify its influence in Western institutions, using the Palestinian cause to gain legitimacy and to press for cultural and political concessions. As we will explore in later chapters, this unholy alliance—between the radical left's ideological zeal and Islam's theological rage—has transformed the Palestinian cause into a global weapon: a coordinated assault on the West's moral and cultural foundations, fueled by a shared obsession with dismantling the so-called "oppressor."

However, with Islam linked to more than 64,000 terrorist attacks in over seventy countries in the twenty-five years since 9/11,[22] the radical left faced a dilemma. If Islam was openly connected to terrorism—and if the Palestinian cause was understood as an Islamic cause—then one of their strongest symbols of "anti-colonial resistance" would collapse. To preserve the Palestinian cause as a rallying banner, a linguistic solution was devised. With the help of Muslim advocates, the term *Islamism* was repurposed and given new meaning: no longer a neutral synonym for Islam, it now served as a dividing line, separating "ordinary Muslims" from those pursuing political or militant agendas. This allowed leftist academics, policymakers, and activists to protect Islamic support for Palestine from being tainted by association with terrorism. By creating a false dichotomy between Islam and *Islamism,* the left and its Muslim allies shielded the faith from scrutiny, ensuring that the Palestinian cause could flourish as a sanctified emblem of resistance, disconnected from the theology that actually sustains it.

After converting to Christianity in 2007, I could no longer safely practice my faith in Jordan. I relocated to Lebanon, where I spent the next fifteen years serving as regional director for the Middle East with a global Christian organization that operates in more than 170 countries, overseeing its work across eight Arab nations. Yet despite the scope of the mission, I had to keep a low profile. Openly expressing my views on Islam or regional politics would have put my life—and those around me—in danger. In 2023, after the birth of my child, with pressure from Jordanian intelligence escalating, and Hezbollah's growing dominance in Lebanon, my wife and I decided to move to the United States. My plan was to continue nonprofit work while quietly building a platform to comment on Islam and Middle Eastern affairs.

But October 7 changed everything.

After witnessing the horrifying response to the massacre—where Islamic jihad was rebranded in Western cities as "resistance" and a struggle for "freedom"—I knew I could no longer remain silent. The very ideology I had fled was now infiltrating the West. I felt compelled to speak out, to warn this civilization about the suicidal path it was on. Yet almost without realizing it, I found myself defending Israel—relentlessly, unapologetically.

The truth is, I never set out to defend Israel. That was not the plan. But somewhere along the way it became clear that this is a civilizational war—a clash between truth and falsehood, liberty and tyranny, light and darkness. And the weight of that global struggle has narrowed into a single, undeniable fault line: Israel versus Islamic jihad. Like it or not, the world is being forced to choose a side. Israel is not just a country; it is the spearhead of the West. And Islam is the driving ideological force seeking to replace the foundations of Western civilization.

In October 2024, I began publishing near-daily pieces on X, focusing on Islam's theological foundations, the real drivers of the Arab-Israeli conflict, and the narratives pushing the West toward collapse. Within just a few months, the response far exceeded anything I had imagined: more than 70,000 people—including policymakers, academics, journalists, and ordinary citizens—began following and engaging with my work.

This book is the product of that momentum. It is a direct response to the flood of questions, the urgency of the moment, and the growing demand for clarity. It is not a casual overview of Islam, nor a political pamphlet. It is a forensic and unapologetic inquiry into the ideological architecture of a political theology masquerading as a religion. The aim is not simply to explain what Muslims believe, but to show what Islam produces— institutionally, psychologically, and geopolitically.

In the chapters ahead, we trace Islam from its theological roots to its role in shaping the Arab-Israeli conflict, and we examine why its worldview is irreconcilable with the West's moral and political order. We expose how language has been manipulated to shield Islam from scrutiny, and why the idea of a shared "Abrahamic" heritage is a dangerous illusion. The book concludes with a collection of selected essays that expand the argument into related arenas, engaging wider cultural and geopolitical debates that flow from the same civilizational struggle.

This is not a book about fearing Muslims, nor is it a book of mere information about Islam. This is a book about defending civilization—the civilization my current faith gave to the world, from the destruction my former faith inflicted on the civilization of my ancestors. It is about knowing what made the West, and what threatens to unmake it. It is about reclaiming the moral confidence to defend what works, and the courage to name what doesn't. This book is for those who are tired of the lies and tired of feeling forced to tolerate what will end the world as they know it, and unwilling to pretend that all stories are equally good. Because some stories built the freedom and dignity we cherish. And some are still trying to burn it down.

Danny Burmawi

ISLAM, ISRAEL AND THE WEST

CHAPTER 1
WHAT IS ISLAM?

THE SACRED ORDER BENEATH IT ALL

From the earliest moments of consciousness, human beings have looked to the heavens, to the rhythms of the seasons, to birth and death, suffering and joy, and asked: *What is behind this? Who am I within it?* Theology begins here, not as dogma but as orientation—the instinct to seek coherence, to interpret the invisible, and to make moral sense of existence.

But this raw impulse must be shaped. It requires language. It requires stories. It requires authority. And so theology crystallizes through narrative. It is encoded in origin myths, epics, hymns, rituals, sacred laws, and divine names. A society's theology emerges not simply from individual contemplation but from what it collectively chooses to remember, repeat, and revere. What it fears. What it blesses. What it believes the gods—or God—require. Over time, these narratives form belief. They are taught to children, inscribed in temples, enforced by kings. And eventually they cease to be remembered as responses to mystery; they are declared as reality itself. This is how theology becomes civilization's bedrock. Its truths are no longer argued; they are assumed. No longer explored; they are enforced. Theology emerges from wonder, is refined through story, and solidified by tradition—until it becomes the order beneath which all else is built.

Because of this, every civilization carries a theological foundation, even when it is not named as such. These ultimate convictions form the moral architecture of a society, determine its direction, and set its boundaries. Behind every renaissance, every revolution, and every collapse lies a vision of the world—and of the ultimate order that gives it meaning, whether named as God or conceived in secular terms.

In the earliest civilizations, theology and power were inseparable. In Mesopotamia, kings ruled by divine sanction;[1] in Egypt, the pharaoh was regarded as the god incarnate. Law, economy, and daily life were all downstream from cosmology. Justice was not an abstract concept but the maintenance of cosmic balance as decreed by the gods.[2] The rise of empires was read as divine favor, their downfall as divine judgment. For these ancient peoples, religion and politics were not two spheres that could be separated—they were a single fabric. Their theology was their philosophy, their governing worldview, and it defined the meaning of their existence.[3]

The Greco-Roman world carried this fusion forward in new ways. What we now call "philosophy" did not emerge in opposition to religion but as its child. The gods of

Olympus did not merely govern the heavens; they animated the moral imagination of the people. The earliest philosophical questions about man and life arose within a cosmos already assumed to be ordered by higher powers. Socrates, Plato, and Aristotle did not begin their inquiries by rejecting the gods, but by asking what kind of cosmos the gods had made and what kind of human life would be worthy within it.[4] Reason was not a rebellion against the sacred but a means of refining its understanding. Philosophy, in this sense, was theology seeking clarity.

Rome inherited and reshaped this synthesis. Greek philosophical categories were absorbed into Roman civic religion, sacralizing law, elevating citizenship, and presenting order itself as a divine mandate. Roman law was not just pragmatic; it was an extension of sacred order, a reflection of divine stability imposed upon the chaos of the world.[5]

Judaism was the first great rupture in ancient religious thought. It introduced a sovereign Creator, transcendent yet just, who established a moral order and declared that every human being—regardless of status or origin—was made in the image of God.[6] This was an ontological revolution. Human dignity was no longer earned or granted by the state; it was inherent.

Christianity built upon this foundation, universalized it, and carried it across cultures and continents. It unveiled the fullness of God's nature—not only as just and sovereign, but also as relational, incarnational, and redemptive. The justice of God was now joined by grace. The sacred was no longer confined to temples or elites; it entered the world through a child in a manger, through fishermen, tax collectors, and outcasts. Christianity made explicit what Judaism had inaugurated: that human value is not tied to bloodline, tribe, or empire, but to creation itself.

This idea—that all people are equal before God—did not remain a doctrine. It erupted into history. It upended empires. Over centuries, it inspired the abolition of slavery, the sanctity of life, the defense of the poor, the elevation of women, and the moral architecture of human rights. It laid the foundation for modern democracies. It gave civilization a new moral center: the worth of the individual. From Jerusalem to Geneva, from Antioch to Philadelphia, the Judeo-Christian vision became the bedrock of the modern world. Wherever it took root, it transformed not only how people prayed but how they governed.

But that transformation was not instant. For centuries, the Church itself became the new institution of power. Its politics shaped monarchies, markets, and daily life. Yet even its corruptions could not fully suppress the revolutionary force embedded in its core doctrines. Eventually, the tension between power and principle erupted. The Reformation shattered the monopoly of sacred interpretation and unleashed the modern West. It was the religious revolution Luther led in Wittenberg that inspired a political one, as townspeople who first broke from the Church soon challenged the civic authority of the Holy Roman Empire itself.[7]

The printing press was a philosophical earthquake. For the first time, ideas moved faster than armies. As theology cracked open, philosophy surged forward. The Enlightenment did not discard religion; it unleashed its consequences. The conviction that man could reason morally apart from clerical control, that conscience could challenge kings, that nature itself was governed by law—all of this emerged from the fusion of Judeo-Christian theology and Greek philosophy.

These ideas did not remain in books. They gave birth to the American Declaration of Independence and the French Declaration of the Rights of Man. They laid the groundwork for human rights, limited government, and constitutional democracy.[8]

But the same power that builds can also destroy. When theology goes unchallenged, or when false gods are enthroned, civilizations deform. Nazi Germany declared that ultimate reality was race. Blood and soil, not human dignity, became the foundation of existence. This was a theological claim: it redefined what it meant to be human. Jews, Slavs, the disabled—these were not just enemies of the state; they were cosmically unworthy. Hitler did not need a god in heaven; he enthroned the Fatherland in its place. Morality was defined not by conscience or transcendence but by the needs of the Volk. The Nazi state was not godless; it had simply made itself god.

Marxist-Leninist communism sought to erase the divine altogether, but in doing so enthroned a new absolute: history itself. Guided by dialectical materialism, history became the author of truth and justice. The Party was its high priest, interpreting the will of the future, purging heretics, promising utopia on the far side of obedience. Morality was no longer anchored in eternal principle but in revolutionary necessity. The family was dismantled, the individual erased. The state became omnipresent, omnipotent, and in its own way, omniscient. It surveilled hearts and minds, punished thought, and demanded conversion—not to God, but to an eschatological fantasy of inevitable communist perfection.

Even postmodernism, which declares that there is no absolute truth, enthrones a god of its own. In denying universality, it divinizes relativism. The individual becomes sovereign, lived experience becomes scripture, and language becomes a sacrament of self-assertion. Those who question this anti-structure are not debated; they are excommunicated. What emerges is not freedom from theology but a new one: a theology of self as god, identity as sacred, and offense as heresy. Even in rebellion against the sacred, postmodernism builds its own altar—one where truth is not denied but privatized and policed.

Whether we admit it or not, every system is theological at its root. Even the claim "there is no god" is a theological claim. It denies one metaphysical order only to enthrone another. The question is never *whether* theology shapes a civilization. The only question is *which theology*—declared or hidden, true or false, liberating or oppressive—is doing the shaping. Strip away the surface of any civilization and you will find a god. Not always named, not always personal, but always present. It may be the state. It may be the race. It may be the collective will, the historical dialectic, or the prophetic leader. But someone, somewhere, is speaking in absolutes. And absolutes always come with rituals, enforcers, doctrines, and consequences.

PRE-ISLAMIC ARABIA

The Arabian Peninsula before Islam was no godless wasteland. It was a spiritual ecosystem, a living theater of theological imagination. Its harsh deserts, violent weather, and unforgiving landscape shaped not only the people's bodies but their vision of the sacred. In a land of fragile agriculture, where survival hinged on tribe, caravan, and season, the divine was not abstract but immediate—encountered in power, proximity, and provision. The gods were tribal guardians, war patrons, fertility figures, and protectors of commerce. They were as real as the sand underfoot, as essential as water, and as territorial as the clans that invoked them. In Arabia, theology was geography. Every valley had its sentinel. Every tribe its chosen god. The sacred was not universal but fractured, not transcendent but local.[9]

The Kaaba in Mecca was the central node in this network, but not the only one. Shrines—*kaabas*—stood in Taif, Sana'a, Dumat al-Jandal, and other places across the region, each sheltering its own idols. Long before Islam, Mecca's sanctuary housed hundreds of deities, each with name, myth, and function. It was a place of worship and arbitration. During sacred months, tribal violence was suspended, and Mecca became a venue for commerce, legal settlements, poetry competitions, marriage alliances, and rituals of purification. Practices such as pilgrimage, circumambulation, fasting, sacrifice, and even ritualized raiding followed sacred calendars and were embedded in the region's theology. Religion was not written on scrolls but etched in stone, timed by the moon, and carried through generations.

Among the most venerated deities was Hubal, chief god of the Quraysh, associated with rain, oracles, and victory in battle. Equally revered were the three great goddesses—al-Lat, al-'Uzza, and Manāt—invoked across tribal lines. Al-Lat governed fertility. Al-'Uzza protected in war. Manāt controlled fate and fortune. These goddesses acted as intercessors with a distant high god often called Allah—not exclusive or personal, but vague, cosmological, absent from daily devotion.[10] Divinity was layered: local gods were near and active, higher gods remote and indifferent. The sacred was utilitarian. The gods protected caravans, judged oaths, and brought rain. Allegiance to deity was inseparable from allegiance to kin. Faith was not orthodoxy but loyalty.

This theological imagination gave Arabia depth, tradition, and identity, but no unity. Every tribe had its god; divine truth was as splintered as the people. The very power of tribal religion made it incapable of transcending tribe. Arabia remained unconquered, but also ungoverned. Rome, Persia, and Byzantium could not absorb it, yet Arabia could not cohere within itself. Trade brought exchange, pilgrimage suspended violence, but no vision bound the tribes beyond survival. The richness of its religion became its ceiling: it preserved but did not evolve, affirmed but did not transcend, bonded but did not unite. The gods were everywhere and nowhere, they tethered the people to fragmentation as much as to faith.

THE CONSOLIDATION OF THE SACRED

As the theological imagination of Arabia reached its limit —rich in ritual, embedded in kinship, but paralyzed by division—a new voice rose from the hills of Mecca. It spoke in the name of one God. But that voice did not emerge from a void. It was not a heavenly interruption upon barren sand. It grew out of the soil it claimed to transcend. Islam was not a break from Arabia's religious past; it was its reassembly.

The longing for unity was real—politically and cosmologically. Tribes were weary of vengeance and fragmentation. Poets had exhausted the old myths. Shrines had multiplied, but none could claim supremacy. Arabia's sacred order was too crowded to carry a single vision forward, yet too revered to be discarded. What was needed was not invention but integration—something powerful enough to unify without appearing foreign. In that tension, Islam found its opening.

Islam in the seventh century was more than a political strategy, but never apart from one. It resolved Arabia's civilizational deadlock by gathering scattered gods under a single banner, centralizing sacred authority in one man, and transforming tribal religion into a system of submission. Its brilliance lay not in creating from nothing, but in fusing what already existed: tribal theology, Arabian ritual, and the hunger for sovereignty.

But unification required legitimacy. A god with no history would be ignored; a theology with no roots would collapse. Muhammad understood this. Allah was already present in Arabia's vocabulary—a distant high god, acknowledged but rarely worshiped.[11] Muhammad did not invent this deity; he elevated him. He stripped the hierarchy of intermediaries and declared Allah alone worthy of worship. The problem, as he framed it, was not that Arabs denied Allah, but that they had betrayed him by invoking others. Familiar language became exclusive allegiance. Still, a high god without narrative was an empty throne. For a backstory, Muhammad turned to Judaism.

Jewish communities had long been present in Medina, Khaybar, and Yemen. They had scripture, prophets, creation accounts, law, and eschatology. They were recognized—even by enemies—as a people of the Book.[12] Muhammad borrowed their framework wholesale. He retold the stories of Adam, Noah, Abraham, Moses, and Joseph. He adopted their terms—Torah, Sabbath, Sheol, shirk. He echoed their dietary laws, mimicked aspects of their prayer cycles, and placed himself within their prophetic arc. This gave Islam narrative depth, wrapping a newborn creed in ancient authority. Allah became not just the god of Arabia, but the God of Abraham. The Kaaba was rebranded as Abraham's sanctuary. Pagan rituals became prophetic commands. Muhammad became not a solitary preacher but the seal of prophecy, superior even to Moses and Jesus.

Yet beneath the monotheistic shell, Arabia remained.[13] The gods were gone, but their functions survived. Tribal loyalty became submission (*Islam*). Military allegiance became jihad. Tribal codes became Sharia. Oral poetry became Qur'an. Islam did not reject Arabia's theological architecture; it institutionalized it.

Nowhere is this clearer than in the infamous incident of the Gharānīq—the "Satanic Verses." Early sources like Ibn Ishaq, al-Tabari, and al-Waqidi recount that, under pressure from Quraysh, Muhammad once recited verses acknowledging the goddesses al-Lat, al-'Uzza, and Manāt: "These are the exalted gharānīq, whose intercession is to be hoped for."[14] The pagans rejoiced. For a moment, reconciliation seemed possible. But Muhammad later retracted the verses, claiming Satan had inspired them. The "revelation" was abrogated. Later scholars tried to suppress the episode, but the impulse it reveals is unmistakable: Muhammad's aim was unity. For the sake of cohesion, he was willing—at least briefly—to make space for the old gods.

Islam was not simply a message; it was a merger. It was not dictated into a vacuum; it was built from existing materials: the narratives of the Jews, the rituals of the pagans, the tribal ethos of Arabia, and the political calculus of survival. It offered not just a god, but a kingdom; not just a prophet, but a sovereign. It replaced many gods with one, and many tribes with one *ummah*. It sanctified war, regulated marriage, standardized inheritance, and monopolized truth. It did what no tribal faith had done: consolidated the sacred into a political order.

For that consolidation to work, the past had to be baptized into the present. The gods had to be replaced but not erased. Rituals preserved, but reinterpreted. Histories hijacked. Myths repurposed. The theology had to appear ancient, the power absolute. Islam was not the creation of a new religion. It was the canonization of Arabia's sacred memory, filtered through borrowed monotheism, aimed at empire.

THE MISSING ELEMENT

Long before Muhammad rose from Mecca with a message of divine unification, another figure emerged from the deserts of Arabia who attempted, in his own way, to reshape the fractured tribal world into a single political body. His name was Kulayb ibn Rabi'ah,[15] a powerful chief of the Banu Taghlib, whose ambition and authority marked one of the earliest recorded attempts to transform Arabia from a tribal mosaic into a centralized monarchy.

Kulayb was no ordinary tribal leader. He had traveled south into Yemen's settled kingdoms and glimpsed what structured rule could look like. The monarchies of Yemen impressed upon him a vision of something beyond lineage and revenge, a vision of rule, border, and crown. He did not want to lead a tribe; he wanted to found a kingdom. And for a time, it looked as if he might succeed.

He consolidated authority across northern Arabia, asserting himself not as a negotiator among equals but as a sovereign above them. He fortified his power with visible symbols of permanence: a stronghold, a settled seat of power, surrounded by walls—unlike the tents of his contemporaries. This alone was radical in a culture where mobility was sacred. But even more radical was his decision to prohibit tribal raids, the lifeblood of the desert economy and a ritual of honor embedded in Arab theology.

Raiding (*ghazw*) was not simply opportunistic theft. It

was tradition, structured by unwritten codes. It redistributed wealth, affirmed valor, and provided cohesion. For young men, it was a rite of passage. For tribes, it was a means of asserting power without total war. For gods, it was a form of sacrifice. By outlawing raids, Kulayb was disrupting the sacred rhythm of life. His prohibition was seen not as order, but as arrogance. His walls were read not as protection, but as pride. He governed by decree but offered no theological framework to sanctify his authority. His kingship was modeled after foreign monarchies, not rooted in Arab sacred memory. He offered a new structure but failed to embed it in a new myth. In a land where theology and kinship were inseparable, he tried to rule by power alone.

The collapse came, as it often does in Arabia, over a camel. Al-Basūs, a woman of the Banu Bakr, brought her prized she-camel into Kulayb's territory. Claiming exclusive rights over the grazing land, Kulayb killed the animal. To him, it was an assertion of law. To the tribes, it was an affront to the gods, to hospitality, to ancestral covenant. The incident triggered the Basus War, a forty-year blood feud that began with a camel and a king's death.

Kulayb was assassinated by his own brother-in-law, Jassas ibn Murrah, in a revenge killing that symbolized more than personal betrayal. It was the tribal order reasserting itself against centralized power that had failed to speak in sacred terms. Kulayb's dream died with him. His walls did not save him. His vision of kingdom collapsed into dust. His story became a cautionary tale, recited in the poetry of lament. He had tried to unify a people through force and structure, but he had ignored the spiritual grammar of the land he sought to govern.

Kulayb failed because he offered Arabia a political structure without sacred legitimacy. Muhammad failed for the first ten years because he offered sacred claims without political power. The two men, separated by a century, fell at opposite ends of the same truth: in Arabia, neither power without the sacred nor the sacred without power could unite a people.

Muhammad began his public mission in Mecca around 613 CE with a bold theological claim: that there was only one God, Allah, and that he, Muhammad, was His final messenger. He challenged the authority of the tribal gods, condemned idol worship, and warned of a coming judgment. His call to exclusive submission sounded, to many, like a demand to surrender power—not to a rival tribe or stronger warrior, but to an unseen authority with no earthly army.

Though his message echoed the familiar rhythms of fear, loyalty, and sacred duty, it arrived without tribal backing, military strength, or enforceable law. In a culture where power was visible, honor was inherited, and strength was existential, such a message, however familiar in form, was perceived as weakness. What Muhammad offered was perceived as a surrender of agency. He spoke of submission, not power; of unseen authority, not tribal might. And in a move that would prove strategically costly, he directed his prayers toward Jerusalem rather than the Kaaba.

The result was a disconnect. He had no ground to rule, no army to enforce, no tribe to defend him. He had only verses. And in a culture where power was public, not promised, that wasn't enough. The tribes of Mecca tolerated him, then slowly began to isolate him. His early followers were mostly the poor, the enslaved, and the marginal—politically inconsequential and socially irrelevant. His own tribe, Banu Hashim, protected him out of kinship obligation,[16] not conviction. But when his uncle Abu Talib died, even that fragile shield began to crack. His movement was weak, his followers scattered, and the city's elite simply waited for his voice to disappear. And it nearly did.

If Muhammad had remained in Mecca preaching faith and condemnation without an alternative center of power, he would have been remembered, if at all, as a failed preacher with grand claims and no ground. But then came the *Hijra*—the migration to Yathrib, later known as Medina. There, Muhammad was no longer a mere prophet; he became a political leader.

The Constitution of Medina established him not just as a spiritual voice, but as the head of a pluralistic city-state.[17] He was now a ruler. With that came the authority to govern, to punish, to legislate, and to protect. It was in Medina that Muhammad recalibrated his strategy. The Kaaba, once the center of idolatry, was reimagined as the original sanctuary of Abraham. The *qibla*, once directed toward Jerusalem, was turned back toward Mecca.[18] The rituals of pilgrimage were reclaimed. The sacred months were reinstated. And the structure of tribal raiding was revived under a new name: jihad.

Raids were launched on Quraysh caravans. Battles ensued. Blood was now spilled in the name of Allah. The theological message had not changed, but its force had. The revelation had found a sword.

This merger of divine authority and worldly power was the turning point. Islam was no longer a message that threatened to tear down the Arab tribes; it became one that reinforced them. The tribes who once mocked Muhammad now saw their rituals restored, their honor affirmed, and their territorial logic embedded in a larger religious framework. Islam became a familiar continuation, rebranded under the name of Allah.

Muhammad succeeded because he finally offered the Arabs something they could understand: the sacred fused with sovereignty. By the time Mecca fell without a fight, and the idols were shattered at the Kaaba, the city that once expelled the prophet now bowed to him. Not because they had all suddenly become monotheists in belief, but because they recognized in his message something they could finally accept: political and economic empowerment, and the preservation of cultural continuity.

Muhammad succeeded where Kulayb failed because he completed the equation. He didn't just offer a god; he offered their world, sanctified. He didn't just propose revelation; he reinforced power. His vision of Allah did not float above Arabia. It descended into it. It looked like Arabia, spoke its language, followed its seasons, used its law, rewarded its warriors, preserved its structures, and simply replaced its names.

In the end, Muhammad triumphed because he created a god in Arabia's image: sovereign, jealous, tribal, merciful to the loyal, and merciless to the enemy. He unified the divided by baptizing their traditions in divine fire. The revelation did not abolish the past; it absorbed it. It carried with it the ghosts of tribal gods, reassembled, repurposed, and recast under the singular will of one God and one prophet.

THE MESSENGER WHO BECAME THE MESSAGE

Muhammad's migration to Medina (*Hijra*) in 622 CE marks more than a geographic or political turning point. It represents a seismic shift in the structure of Islamic authority itself. In Mecca, Muhammad claimed the role of a *nadhir* (warner), a prophet crying out in the wilderness, issuing eschatological warnings to a polytheistic society entrenched in tribal religiosity. But in Medina, his status evolved dramatically. With military power, economic control, and legislative authority now in his hands, Muhammad ceased to be merely the messenger of the message. He became its embodiment, its sole interpreter, and its center.

From this moment forward, Islamic praxis developed what might be described as a functional binitarianism: Allah remained ultimate in theory, but Muhammad became the necessary mediator, interpreter, and access point through whom divine will was revealed and enforced. While Islam formally rejects the Christian Incarnation, in practice it elevated Muhammad to a status not entirely unlike that of Christ—not divine, but indispensable.

This centrality is most evident in how Muhammad's biography (*sira*) and actions (*sunnah*) eclipse the Qur'an in shaping Islamic law and moral consciousness.[19] The Qur'an alone is insufficient to establish rulings. It is the hadith corpus—records of his words (*qawl*), deeds (*fiʿl*), and tacit approvals (*taqrīr*)—that forms the primary tool of jurisprudence. In practice, Islamic law is not Qur'an-centric but Prophet-centric.

Even the Qur'an itself reflects this transformation. The early Meccan surahs are poetic, apocalyptic, and theocentric, focused on God's majesty and the call to monotheism. The Medinan surahs, however, shift toward legalism, community organization, warfare, and submission to the authority of the Prophet.[20] Surah 4:80 asserts, *"Whoever obeys the Messenger has obeyed Allah,"* effectively fusing prophetic authority with divine command. Surah 33:36 tells believers they have no choice but to obey Muhammad's decisions, even in personal matters. Revelation increasingly addressed his own circumstances, conflicts, and vindications. Unlike biblical prophets, who pointed beyond themselves with, *"Thus says the Lord,"* Muhammad's authority folded back onto himself.

In the biblical model, the prophet is a vessel, not the message itself. The authority of prophecy lies not in the messenger's perfection but in God's word. The Hebrew Bible recounts with ruthless honesty the failures of its prophets: Moses' disobedience, David's adultery, Jonah's rebellion, Elijah's despair. Their imperfections do not disqualify them, because authority resides in the divine source, not in the man. The message stands above the messenger.

The New Testament continues this pattern. The apostles are not presented as flawless interpreters of doctrine. Peter denies Christ. Thomas doubts. Paul rebukes Peter publicly. Their weakness does not undermine the gospel; it underscores that the gospel does not depend on them. Even the later founders of Christian traditions are not beyond critique: Luther's anti-Semitism is condemned by Lutherans,[21] Calvin's role in the death of Servetus is rejected by Presbyterians. In Judaism and Christianity, the man serves the text. In Islam, the text serves the man.

This reversal shapes the entire Islamic system. The Qur'an is believed to have descended verbatim in a fixed linguistic form, unmediated by human shaping. Yet its meaning is inseparable from Muhammad's life. *Tafsir* (exegesis), *usul al-fiqh* (jurisprudential principles), and *sira* (biography) do not interpret the Qur'an apart from Muhammad; they interpret it through him. This framework eliminates interpretive elasticity. The Qur'an cannot be read in abstraction, subjected to historical-critical inquiry, or philosophically reconstructed. Its authoritative reading is already embedded in Muhammad's life. His words and deeds are the interpretive grid, and that grid is fixed. If he laughed, hadith preserves it. If he slept a certain way, legal manuals record it. If he punished an enemy, that act becomes precedent. The Prophet is not simply the messenger; he is the message as lived reality.

This has profound consequences. If Muhammad made war, war is sanctified. If he ordered assassinations, those are jurisprudential precedents. If he expressed hostility toward Jews or Christians, that hostility becomes doctrine. The Sunnah records his campaigns, his treatment of captives, his treaty-making, his punishments, and his judgments in disputes. These are not anecdotes; they are templates. The hadith literature, authenticated through chains of transmission and integrated into every facet of jurisprudence, ensures his example is ever-binding.

This explains Islam's distinctive sensitivities. Across the Muslim world, blasphemy laws exist not to protect Allah, but to guard Muhammad's honor. Cartoons of God provoke little reaction. Cartoons of Muhammad provoke riots. The earliest assassinations ordered by his followers were not against idolaters but against poets who mocked him personally: Ka'b ibn al-Ashraf, Asma bint Marwan, Abu Afak, and others. The offense was not rejection of God but insult to the Prophet.[22]

Islamic soteriology confirms this orientation. Jews and Christians—monotheists who affirm the God of Abraham—are nonetheless condemned in the Qur'an as *kuffar*. Not because they deny God, but because they deny Muhammad. Surah 4:150–151 declares that those who "believe in Allah but not in His Messenger" are the most misguided. The *Shahada* makes this explicit: "There is no god but Allah, and Muhammad is His messenger." Without Muhammad's name, God's name is inert. No other prophet in the Abrahamic tradition demanded such allegiance. Moses never said, "Reject me and burn." Even Jesus pointed beyond himself to the Father.

The result is a theological structure where Allah is distant, unknowable, terrifying, and abstract, while Muhammad is proximate, emotional, imitable, and ever-present. Devotion centers not on the divine, but on the man who claimed to reveal it. His decisions, habits, and silences are all binding. His will becomes law. His person becomes the lens of revelation.

This is why Islam cannot be apolitical if Muhammad was political. And he was. His community was not a church; it was a state. Every major domain of Islamic governance (*siyasa*), warfare (*jihad*), taxation (*zakat, jizya*), punishment (*hudud*), and treaty-making (*'ahd*) finds precedent in his actions. The command to fight disbelievers until they submit (Qur'an 9:29) is not merely textual; it is historical. Muhammad did not only preach jihad; he led it. He did not merely warn against dissent; he ordered executions. He did not only urge submission; he enforced it.

In this sense, Islam is not simply the preservation of a message. It is the institutionalization of a life. Muslims are not called to obey abstract principles but to emulate a man whose every decision is sacred precedent. Muhammad is not symbolic; he is supreme authority who forms the canon.

This makes Islam structurally different from Judaism and Christianity. The fallibility of biblical prophets preserved the sovereignty of revelation. In Islam, to critique Muhammad is to attack the religion itself. The man and the message are indivisible.

This fusion transforms Islam from a religion into an ideology. When the messenger becomes inseparable from the message, worship shifts from transcendent devotion to immanent enforcement. The sacred is no longer vertical— lifting the soul toward the divine—but horizontal, policed through community, politics, and coercion. What results is not a faith that liberates, but an ideology that governs, demanding allegiance, regulating society, and measuring salvation by submission to authority.

THE ANATOMY OF A POLITICAL IDEOLOGY

The concept of *ideology* has been one of the most contested in political theory. Since its coining by Destutt de Tracy in the late eighteenth century as a "science of ideas,"[23] it has carried shifting connotations. However, Stanford Encyclopedia of Philosophy defines a political ideology as a "set of beliefs and principles that form a comprehensive worldview on how society should be organized and governed. It provides a blueprint for a preferred social and economic order by explaining how things are, how they ought to be, and what methods are best to achieve that ideal state."[24]

This makes political ideology more than philosophy or belief. It carries a program for power. It translates ideas into institutions, doctrines into laws, convictions into coercion. Unlike private religion, a political ideology demands public obedience and embeds its principles into the fabric of society. Its architecture can be recognized through three defining elements:[25]

(1) **Core Values**: a system of belief that governs all spheres of life.

(2) **Political Goals**: a strategic vision for power and expansion.

(3) **Strategies**: mechanisms of institutional enforcement

Wherever all three converge, the line between religion

and political ideology collapses—and it is here that Islam must be examined.

1. Core Values:

Political ideologies begin with axioms—claims of truth that structure how reality is interpreted. In Marxism, this is the struggle between classes; in liberalism, the sovereignty of the individual. Islam's foundational axiom is the absolute sovereignty of Allah (*tawhid*), which is not confined to metaphysics or theology. The Qur'an, Hadith, and subsequent Islamic legal tradition make it clear that this sovereignty must manifest itself in governance, legislation, and judicial authority (Qur'an 12:40).

2. Political Goal

The Qur'an repeatedly emphasizes the duty to establish Allah's rule on earth (hukm Allah), as seen in verses such as 9:33: *"It is He who sent His Messenger with guidance and the religion of truth to manifest it over all religion."* This is not symbolic. It is expansionist in design and strategic in execution. The concept of *Dar al-Islam* (the abode of submission) versus *Dar al-Harb* (the abode of war)[26] illustrates that Islam is not content to remain a private faith; it defines itself in terms of jurisdiction and territorial reach.

3. Strategy

Finally, Islam established institutional mechanisms to enforce its vision. This is made explicit in sacred texts such as Qur'an 9:29

> *"Fight those who do not believe in Allah nor in the Last Day, who do not forbid what Allah and His Messenger have forbidden, and who do not embrace the religion of truth, from among the People of the Book, until they pay the jizya with willing*

submission and feel themselves subdued." Also Quran 8:39 *"Fight them until there is no more fitnah [disbelief or resistance], and religion is entirely for Allah."*

Here, non-compliance is not merely condemned—it is met with sanctioned coercion: conversion, political subjugation through the jizya tax, or war. Classical commentators such as al-Qurtubi emphasize that this command is absolute, not confined to any particular time, place, or people. In other words, it establishes a permanent principle of enforcement.[27]

Unlike Christianity, whose sacred texts do not prescribe a political order and whose early church spread apart from state power, Islam's institutional form was conceived from the outset within the apparatus of the state. The first four Caliphs (*Rashidun*), particularly Abu Bakr and Umar, fused military, judicial, and legislative authority into one office. Later, the Umayyad and Abbasid dynasties expanded this into bureaucratic empires, employing legal scholars (*ulama*), judges (*qadis*), and state muftis to consolidate rule under theocratic auspices. Islamic law was not simply applied by the state, it was the state.

And unlike Judaism, which developed the Talmud as a vast code addressing nearly every aspect of life, Islam added what Judaism never claimed: universality. The Talmud orders life for a covenantal people within a particular land, but it does not envision a global mission. Christianity, by contrast, carried such a universal ethic—embodied in the Golden Rule and the call to preach to all nations—yet it lacked a political blueprint. Islam fused what the others kept separate: comprehensive law, universal expansion, and institutional enforcement.

This is the signature of a political ideology.

Comparative Anatomy of Religions and Ideologies

Tradition / Ideology	Core Values[1]	Political Goal[2]	Strategy[3]
Islam	✓	✓	✓
Christianity	✗	✓ (spiritual)	✗
Judaism	✓	✗	✗
Marxism	✓	✓	✓
Liberalism	✓	✓	✓
Conservatism	✓	✓	✓
Anarchism	✓	✓ ("chaos")	✓ (revolution)

THE ENDURING SHADOW OF THE ISLAMIC STATE

If ideology is a belief system that not only explains the world but seeks to dominate it through organized authority, then history becomes its most powerful witness. In the case of Islam, its political aspirations cannot be separated from its historical trajectory. From the death of Muhammad in 632 CE until the abolition of the Ottoman Caliphate in 1924, the *ummah* lived under a continuous political structure that asserted not merely a religious identity but legal authority, territorial governance, military expansion, and socio-political hierarchy. This unbroken lineage is the spine of Islamic history. The Islamic state was not an intermittent experiment; it was a continuous, institutionalized reality.

Initially centered in Medina, it expanded under the Rightly Guided Caliphs, assumed imperial form under the Umayyads, developed administrative sophistication under the Abbasids, defended its realm through the Seljuks and Mamluks, and extended global reach under the Ottomans. Dynastic names and administrative forms varied, but the essential aim never changed: to preserve and implement Allah's law over society. Whether through the conquests of Khalid ibn al-Walid or the bureaucratic decrees of the *Shaykh al-Islam* in Istanbul, the Islamic state functioned as the vessel of divine governance itself.

This continuity explains one of the defining traits of Islamic history: crises were rarely defined by lapses in spiritual fervor, but by the loss of state power. A decline in piety might invite sermons, but a decline in sovereignty invited despair. For Islamic civilization, legitimacy was never derived primarily from moral perfection but from the state's ability to uphold Sharia,* maintain order, and extend Islamic control.[28] This is why rulers with dubious personal conduct—whether the Umayyads or later Abbasids—were still recognized as legitimate: they governed in the name of Islam. Jurists might criticize their ethics, but they rarely denied their authority. Ibn Khaldun articulated this reality in the 14th century: *"The strength of religion is dependent upon the strength of the state."* The state was not incidental to the faith; it was its necessary vehicle.[29]

---

* **Sharia:** the body of Islamic law derived from the Qur'an, the hadith (traditions of Muhammad), and centuries of juristic interpretation. It covers both personal religious practice and social, political, and legal matters.

From the early caliphs to the Ottoman sultans, governance was the tangible manifestation of Islam's claim over all domains of life. This governing legacy ended in 1924 when Mustafa Kemal Atatürk formally abolished the Ottoman Caliphate.[30] It was not simply the termination of a political office but the rupture of a fourteen-century-old assumption that Islam must rule. The caliphate had already been weakened through European colonial incursions and Ottoman reform, but its symbolic dismantling struck a blow at the heart of Islamic identity. For centuries, Muslims had believed that however fragmented the *ummah* became, a central polity still embodied their collective submission to Allah. With the Caliphate's abolition, that belief collapsed.

Across the Islamic world, the event was seen as a theological catastrophe. It was interpreted as the suspension of God's presence in history, a void where divine authority no longer had a representative on earth. From that point forward, movements of every kind—pietistic, revivalist, and militant—emerged to fill the vacuum. Yet the consensus remained: without Islamic governance, Islam itself was incomplete.

CHAPTER 2
THE ISLAMIC WAR ON ISRAEL

THE END OF THE CALIPHATE

At the dawn of the 20th century, the Ottoman Caliphate—though battered by foreign incursions and hollowed by internal reforms—still stood as the symbolic and political embodiment of Islamic sovereignty. For centuries it had served as the unifying authority of the *ummah*, administering territories from Bosnia to Yemen through institutions rooted in Sharia.[1] Yet by the 19th century, the Caliphate's adoption of Western-style reforms, including secular legal codes that curtailed the authority of Sharia, provoked growing disillusionment among Arab Muslims.[2] To many, these reforms were not modernization but betrayal—a violation of the Caliphate's divine mandate.

In the Arab heartlands, particularly in the Hejaz,* calls

---

* **Hejaz:** a region in western Arabia that includes Islam's holiest cities, Mecca and Medina. It was the birthplace of Muhammad and the starting arose to restore the Caliphate to what was imagined as its original purity.³ The Hashemite ruler of Mecca, Sharif Hussein bin Ali—a direct descendant of the Prophet Muhammad—positioned himself as the vessel of this revival. Hussein's vision was ambitious: a reconstituted Caliphate centered in Mecca, ruled by prophetic lineage, governing a vast Arab kingdom stretching from the Hejaz to the Levant, encompassing what would later become Syria, Lebanon, Iraq, Jordan, and Israel.⁴ It was both a political project and a theological claim, promising to preserve the unity of the *ummah* under Islamic law.

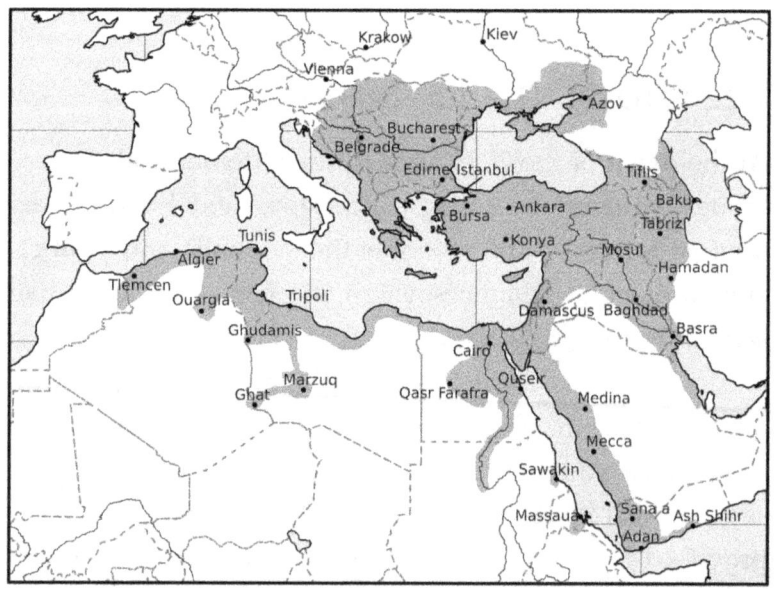

Hussein's aspirations soon converged with the geopo-

---

point of Islamic expansion. Historically, the Hejaz was not a center of advanced civilization — it was a tribal, desert society — but it became central because of Islam's rise and its religious sites.

litical designs of Britain during World War I. Desperate to undermine the Ottomans, the British sought Arab support through the McMahon–Hussein Correspondence (1915–1916), a series of letters now preserved in the UK National Archives.[5] In these exchanges, Sir Henry McMahon, the British High Commissioner in Egypt, pledged support for an independent Arab state in return for Hussein's leadership of a revolt against Ottoman rule. Hussein, however, read these assurances not as a promise of secular independence but as a mandate to restore the Caliphate under Arab stewardship, with himself at its helm.

His language made this religious framing unmistakable.

> "I, Al-Hussein bin Ali, who arose with my people, the Arabs, and the vast majority of those who speak the language of the Arabs, who agreed with my view on the situation of this *ummah*, which was dictated by religious feeling first..."[6]

In a statement to Ronald Storrs, Oriental Secretary to the British High Commissioner in Egypt, Hussein went further: "There no longer exists a Caliphate... for their [the Ottomans'] rule projects... deeds that are all contrary to religion."[7] For Hussein, the Ottoman claim to the Caliphate had already collapsed; the task was not to dissolve the institution but to reclaim it, replacing Turkish custodianship with Arab legitimacy.

This helps explain why the growing Jewish presence in Palestine prior to World War I—waves of legal land purchases, the founding of agricultural colonies, and the construction of new cities between 1882 and 1914—provoked little organized Arab resistance.[8] Zionist institution-building took place within the framework of Ottoman sovereignty, which, though fragile, still carried the sacred legitimacy of the Caliphate. In Arab imagination, the political order was not being rejected but simply awaited restoration through Arab leadership. So long as the land remained under an Islamic sovereign, Jewish settlement was tolerated as subordinate activity within an Islamic polity.

Jewish settlers operated firmly within this Ottoman framework. Land acquisitions were conducted legally through established mechanisms of the empire,[9] often purchased directly from Arab landowners. Their efforts—whether agricultural, educational, or urban—did not, at this stage, pose a theological threat. For the Arabs, the

Caliphate was in transition, but its sovereignty over Palestine remained intact. As long as Jewish activity did not challenge that paradigm of Islamic rule, it was tolerated.

During this period, Jewish pioneers established towns such as Petah Tikva (1878), Rishon LeZion (1882), Zikhron Ya'akov (1882), Rehovot (1890), and Tel Aviv (1909).[10] They drained the malaria-ridden Hula swamps, introduced modern irrigation systems, and transformed barren fields into productive farmland. In a letter to the people of Transjordan, the former mayor of Madaba, Salem Abu Al-Ghanam wrote:

> *"The Zionist nation is renowned across Europe for its productivity and success. By coming here, their aim is to build and to develop, to eradicate disease, and to drain the swamps. We, in turn, will share in the prosperity of what they establish."*[11]

In cities such as Haifa, Jews modernized the port and created new networks of shipping and trade. Institutions of culture and learning also flourished: the Herzliya Hebrew Gymnasium (1905) in Jaffa,[12] the Bezalel School of Arts (1906) in Jerusalem, and the Technion (1912) in Haifa became symbols of a revitalized national life.

The dynamism of these projects generated ripple effects far beyond the Jewish community. Higher wages, employment opportunities, and improved living conditions attracted Arab laborers and migrants from surrounding regions—Egypt, Syria, Lebanon, and Transjordan—who moved into Palestine in search of work.[13] British Mandate–era reports later confirmed this demographic shift. The 1937 Peel Commission noted that "the general beneficent effect of Jewish immigration on Arab welfare is illustrated by the increase in the Arab population,"[14] while the 1930 Hope-Simpson Report explicitly recorded that "immigration from Syria and Transjordan" was driven by "better conditions" created under Jewish development.[15]

Jewish revival in the land was tolerated so long as it remained beneath the banner of Islamic political control. In the minds of Arab leaders and intellectuals, sovereignty was intact and destined to be Arabized, not dismantled. As long as continuity of Islamic authority was preserved— first Ottoman, then potentially Hashemite—the Jewish presence, though scrutinized, was not regarded as a theological rebellion. It was tolerated as progress under permission.[16]

The British, however, had no intention of honoring their promises. Even as they exchanged letters with Hussein through the McMahon-Hussein Correspondence, they were secretly negotiating the Sykes-Picot Agreement (1916) with France, partitioning Ottoman territories into spheres of influence.[17] This agreement smuggled into the Middle East a foreign concept the region had never known: the nation-state. For centuries, the Islamic world had functioned within the universalist framework of the Caliphate, where borders were fluid and identity was defined by religion, not nationality. The imposition of modern nation-states—Lebanon, Syria, Iraq, Jordan, and eventually Israel—fractured the ummah's imagined unity, erecting artificial boundaries that clashed directly with the Islamic vision of a single Caliphate.

THE ROOT OF THE CONFLICT

The fragmentation of the post-Ottoman order was felt most acutely in Mount Lebanon — a historic Christian stronghold that had long operated as a semi-autonomous entity under both the Ottomans and the Egyptians. Yet, despite its Christian character, Muslim communities throughout the Levant still regarded it as unquestionably part of the House of Islam, and therefore Islamic land.[18] That perception was violently disrupted in 1920, when France—acting through General Henri Gouraud and in partnership with Maronite Patriarch Elias Howayek—declared the establishment of Greater Lebanon after seizing Beirut from the Sunnis, who had pledged allegiance to Sharif Hussein's Caliphate.[19] For Muslims, both Sunni and Shia, the creation of an independent Christian-led state on historically Islamic territory, under European Christian protection, was perceived as a direct violation of Islamic sovereignty—at once theologically intolerable and politically illegitimate.[20]

Faced with this rejection, Christian leaders sought to appease Muslim communities in order to legitimize the new state. Patriarch Howayek and other Maronite figures emphasized Lebanon's Arab identity and its affiliation, and pledged to respect Muslim religious and civil rights.[21] The 1926 Lebanese Constitution was presented as a gesture of inclusion, with Sunni and Shia politicians invited to participate in drafting the text. Christian newspapers and political elites framed Lebanon not as a Christian project but as a pluralistic Arab homeland for all sects. Yet these overtures failed to mask the deeper issue: from the Muslim perspective, the very foundation of Lebanon—the separation from the larger Arab-Islamic body and the alignment with Western Christian powers—was a desecration of inherited guardianship over Islamic land.[22]

Lebanon's Christians, determined to preserve their fragile sovereignty in a region dominated by Islamic identity politics, attempted to legitimize their leadership by aligning with Muslim causes. In 1948, Lebanon joined the Arab League's war against the newly established Jewish state, deploying troops alongside Egypt, Syria, and Jordan. Maronite leaders, including President Bechara El Khoury, framed this as Arab solidarity, hoping to disprove suspicions that the Christian-led state was disloyal to the broader ummah. But no gesture, however public, could resolve the core tension. The objection was never about partnership or regional solidarity—it was about sovereignty. For many Muslims, Lebanon was Islamic land, and legitimacy required full submission to Islamic political authority. This was the line Christian leaders could not cross. Their refusal to yield the state's sovereignty, insisting instead on a national identity independent of Islamic rule, made reconciliation structurally impossible.

Unable to confront the issue directly, Muslim leaders often cloaked their theological demand in broader ideological movements. Pan-Arab nationalism in the 1950s and 1960s provided a convenient vehicle to challenge Christian political dominance under the guise of unity and anti-imperialism. Spearheaded by Egypt's Gamal Abdel Nasser, pan-Arabism cast the Arab world as one nation united by language and culture, with Islam as its unspoken backbone.[23] In Lebanon, Sunni and Shia leaders embraced this ideology to undermine the Christian-led state, arguing that Lebanon's sovereignty should be subordinated to the wider Arab cause. But the Arab defeat in the 1967 Six-Day War against Israel discredited pan-Arabism, leaving a vacuum that Palestinianism quickly filled.

In Lebanon, Muslims saw the Palestinian struggle as a new lever to destabilize Christian rule. The 1969 Cairo Agreement between Yasser Arafat and Lebanese General Emile Bustani, brokered by Nasser, granted the PLO control over refugee camps in southern Lebanon and the right to launch attacks against Israel from Lebanese soil.[24] Sunni politicians endorsed the deal as a moral obligation to resist "Zionist aggression." Prime Minister Saeb Salam tied Lebanon's future to Palestinian resistance. In reality, it shifted the power balance: Palestinian militias, armed and autonomous, eroded the Christian-led government's authority. Southern Lebanon became a war zone, Israeli retaliations escalated, and sectarian tensions deepened. By 1975, these tensions exploded into the Lebanese Civil War (1975–1990), pitting Christian militias such as the Kataeb and Lebanese Forces against Muslim and Palestinian factions.

The 1979 Iranian Revolution introduced a new actor: Iran, which identified Lebanon's Shia population as fertile ground for exporting its Islamic revolutionary ideology. In 1982, Iran founded Hezbollah, ostensibly to resist Israel's invasion but with the broader aim of imposing Islamic dominance. Hezbollah's 1985 charter explicitly called for an Islamic state in Lebanon.[25] Its general secretary, Hasan Nasrallah, admitted in a widely circulated video that Hezbollah's true objective was never to preserve

Lebanon's independence but to transform it into a wilayah —an Islamic province—subordinate to the Shia caliphate in Iran.[26]

The 1989 Taif Agreement,[27] which ended the civil war, dealt a decisive blow to Christian authority. Brokered by Saudi Arabia and Syria, it redistributed parliamentary seats, stripped the Christian president of executive powers, and transferred authority to a Sunni prime minister and a Shia speaker of parliament. Celebrated as a compromise, it effectively ended Christian dominance and aligned Lebanon with the Muslim-majority regional order.

Lebanon, once dubbed the "Switzerland of the Middle East"[28] for its cultural vibrancy and economic prosperity, deteriorated into a failed state. Lebanon's Christians paid the price for believing they could coexist with Muslims while maintaining sovereignty. Their decline was not an anomaly but a case study in Islam's uncompromising stance on non-Muslim rule. Christians, like Jews in Palestine, were tolerated as dhimmis under the Caliphate but became targets when they claimed sovereignty.

Across the Islamic world, this pattern repeats with relentless consistency: secular, tribal, or heterodox rulers presiding over Muslim-majority populations face either violent overthrow or universal delegitimization, as their authority is seen as betrayal of the Islamic imperative for supremacy. This dynamic is rooted in the theological conviction that legitimacy derives solely from upholding Islamic governance, a principle that transcends politics. In times of strength, Muslim movements depose such rulers; in times of weakness, they brand them agents of infidels, eroding their legitimacy through ideological warfare. No amount of anti-Zionist posturing, symbolic piety, or deference to Muslim sensibilities can bridge this divide.

Syria under the Assad regime exemplifies this pattern. In 1970, Hafez al-Assad, an Alawite, seized power through a military coup, aligning his Ba'athist regime with Arab nationalism. To Syria's Sunni majority, Alawites were heretics. Assad sought legitimacy through a 1973 fatwa from Shia cleric Musa al-Sadr, who declared Alawites part of Twelver Shiism. Sunnis, however, rejected this and the Muslim Brotherhood escalated resistance. By the late 1970s, riots, assassinations, and insurgency wracked Aleppo and Homs. In 1979, the Muslims Brotherhood massacred 83 Alawite cadets at Aleppo's Artillery School. A year later, they attempted to assassinate Assad. His retaliation was brutal: the 1982 siege of Hama killed between 10,000–40,000 civilians. The rebellion was crushed, but Sunni resentment deepened.[29]

Assad's son, Bashar, inherited this fragile order in 2000. The Arab Spring of 2011 turned protests for reform into armed jihad, spearheaded by groups like Jabhat al-Nusra (al-Qaeda's Syrian affiliate) and later Hay'at Tahrir al-Sham (HTS). These groups framed the conflict as a divine struggle to restore Islamic rule. In 2015, HTS leader Abu Mohammad al-Julani declared on Al Jazeera: "Our goal is to establish the Caliphate, implement Sharia, and liberate Syria from apostate rule." By December 2024, after nearly 14 years of war, HTS captured Damascus, forcing Bashar al-Assad into exile. For the first time in modern history, Syria fell under openly Islamic governance.

This was the culmination of a century-long ideological struggle, driven by the conviction that only Islamic governance is legitimate. The Assad regime's secular Ba'athism, like Lebanon's Christian-led state, was an affront to the ummah's vision of sovereignty. That is why the war on Israel must be understood within the same framework. It is not a dispute over settlements or borders—it is a war against Jewish sovereignty itself.

Just as Lebanon's Christian sovereignty was rejected for daring to rule Islamic land outside Sharia, so too Israel is rejected for daring to exist as a sovereign Jewish nation on territory once claimed by Islam. Israel's emergence forced the Arab world to accept the permanence of the nation-state system. That is why Israel remains an obsession. Erasing it would not just mean the elimination of one small state; it would reopen the path to a caliphate, undo the hard boundary that Israel imposed, and restore the dream of empire.

HIJACKING PALESTINE

For most of recorded history, "Palestine" was a geographical label, not the name of a state or the banner of a distinct people. To project backward the notion that a sovereign Palestinian nation once existed—dispossessed by colonial conspiracies—is historical revisionism of the highest order. The term was never created by Arabs, and certainly not by a people calling themselves Palestinians. It was imposed by conquerors—first by the Romans, then later by the British—as an imperial designation for a region whose population never self-identified as a single nation.

The origin of the word "Palestine" dates to the Roman Emperor Hadrian in 135 CE, after the Jewish Bar Kokhba revolt. In an act of deliberate humiliation, Hadrian renamed the province of Judea to *Syria Palaestina*, borrowing the name from the long-defeated Philistines—historic enemies of Israel—in order to suppress Jewish identity and erase Jewish claims to the land.[30] The name persisted in Byzantine, Islamic, and European writings as a regional term, but never as the title of a state, a government, or a national movement.

By the late 19th and early 20th centuries, under Ottoman rule, the land known today as Israel, the West Bank, and Gaza was not governed as a single entity called Palestine. Instead, it was divided into administrative districts—the Jerusalem Sanjak,* and parts of the Beirut and Damascus Vilayets. †,[31] There was no Palestinian authority, no parliament, no flag, no capital city bearing that name. Only after the fall of the Ottoman Empire in World War I did the term reemerge—this time under British control—as an administrative convenience, not a recognition of national identity. The League of Nations Mandate for Palestine, granted to Britain in 1922, codified the term in law. The mandate explicitly called for the establishment of "a national home for the Jewish people" while safeguarding the civil and religious rights of existing non-Jewish communities. Nowhere did it recognize, nor even hint at, a sovereign Arab state of Palestine. Arab leaders across the region knew this well. Their resistance was not

---

* **Sanjak:** an administrative district in the Ottoman Empire, smaller than a province. Several sanjaks together formed a vilayet.

† **Vilayet:** a large administrative province in the Ottoman Empire, governed by a vali (provincial governor) and typically made up of several sanjaks.

to defend a uniquely Palestinian identity but to reject Jewish sovereignty altogether.

What did emerge under the British Mandate were emblems of governance: passports, coins, stamps, and official seals bearing the word "Palestine." Yet these should not be misread as signs of national existence. They were colonial tools, as politically empty as stamps marked "British India" or "French Indochina." Passports labeled "Palestine" were issued by British consulates and carried equally by Jews and Arabs. The Palestinian Citizenship Order of 1925 merely confirmed that all Ottoman subjects in the territory would henceforth be "citizens of Palestine" under British authority.

Indeed, Jewish institutions freely used the word "Palestine" during the Mandate, not because they identified as "Palestinian" in the modern Arab sense, but because it was the internationally recognized name of the territory. The *Palestine Post*—today's *Jerusalem Post*—was a Jewish newspaper. The Palestine Philharmonic Orchestra, now the Israel Philharmonic, was founded by Jewish refugees from Nazi Germany. The Jewish Agency referred to its work "in Palestine."[32] Palestine Airways Limited and the Palestine Electric Corporation were both Jewish-owned enterprises. Jewish products carried the label "Made in Palestine," just as goods made in Alaska before 1959 bore "Made in U.S. Territory."

Arab nationalists did not object to this terminology, because at the time "Palestinian" was not a national identifier. The Arab press itself referred to Jews as Palestinians, just as it spoke of Jaffa citrus or Haifa textiles as "Palestinian" exports. When Arab activists organized economic boycotts, they called them boycotts of "Palestinian products." Tellingly, there was no Palestinian flag, no Palestinian parliament, and no Palestinian government throughout this period. Arabs in the land were absorbed into broader Arab nationalist and pan-Islamic movements; their loyalties were to Damascus, Cairo, Baghdad—or to Islam itself—not to a distinct Palestinian nation.

When Arab armies invaded the nascent State of Israel in 1948, they did not march under a Palestinian banner. They fought under the flags of Egypt, Syria, Jordan, Iraq, and Lebanon. Their aim was not to "liberate Palestine" as a sovereign homeland, but to annihilate the Jewish state.

The 1948 Arab-Israeli War marked a decisive turning point. With Israel's declaration of independence—secured legally, diplomatically, and militarily—the old British administrative label of "Palestine" was vacated. Into that vacuum, a new narrative was born. For the first time, the term *Palestinian* began to acquire the weight of national identity.

In the years that followed, the Arab world confronted a propaganda dilemma: how to delegitimize a Jewish state that had emerged within the framework of international law and United Nations recognition. The solution was retroactive invention. A displaced and oppressed "Palestinian nation" was conjured into history, supposedly predating Israel. Yet before 1948, not a single international resolution, not a single Arab League charter, and not a single local declaration referred to a sovereign Palestinian nation. The identity was not preserved from antiquity—it was constructed after the fact.

What emerged were political tools, symbols masquerading as heritage. The Palestinian flag, for example, was not of Palestinian origin at all. It derived from the banner of the Arab Revolt of 1916, later used by the short-lived Arab Federation of Iraq and Jordan in 1958, and finally co-opted by the Palestine Liberation Organization in 1964.[33] Its design is shared by Jordan, Sudan, Kuwait, and the former United Arab Republic. There is nothing uniquely Palestinian about it.

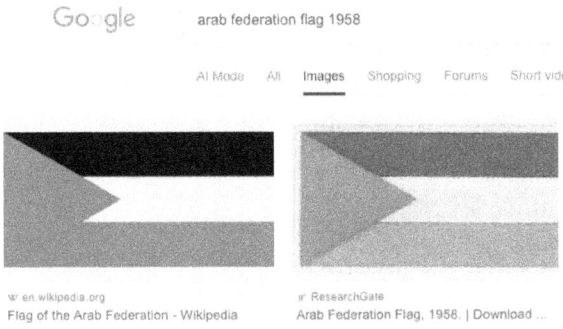

Unlike nations such as Lebanon or Syria, which emerged with borders, capitals, constitutions, and functioning bureaucracies, the so-called Palestinian state has no historical parallel. The Palestinian identity, as understood today, was not the continuity of an ancient people but the product of defeat—a reactionary identity forged in the crucible of conflict, defined not by its own achievements, but by opposition to Jewish sovereignty.

This is not to deny that Arab families lived in the land for centuries, or to erase the memories of those who once dwelled in Haifa, Acre, or Hebron. But lineage and nostalgia do not constitute nationhood. Across the Middle East, millions of Arabs trace their ancestry to particular towns, villages, or tribes—yet not every village becomes a state. The claim that "Palestine" was hijacked by Israel inverts reality. It was the Arab world that hijacked the label, transforming it from a neutral geographic term into a weaponized political narrative.

Here lies the great irony. The Jews of Mandatory Palestine fought against the British Empire for national independence, much as Christians in Lebanon or Arabs in Syria resisted French colonialism. Those struggles culminated in the birth of sovereign states. But the Jewish victory, alone among them, was denied legitimacy by its neighbors. The Arab world accepted independence for Iraq, Syria, and Jordan—but not for Israel. Why? Because Israel was not Islamic. The rejection of Jewish sovereignty was absolute.

Unable to reverse the facts on the ground, Arab leaders turned instead to linguistic and historical appropriation. They seized the only label available—*Palestine*—and infused it with new meaning. What had been the British Mandate's administrative shorthand became, retroactively, the name of an allegedly ancient people. The rejection of partition was reframed as resistance to displacement. The denial of peace was rebranded as a cry for justice. Thus a convenient narrative was born: the Jews had stolen "Palestine," and the Palestinians simply wanted it back.

NOMINALISM

In the classical philosophical sense, nominalism is the idea that names (nomina) are not realities in themselves but mere labels attached to things. In other words, the *name* does not necessarily reflect an independent essence—it's a designation, a convenience, a construct. Applied politically, nominalism means the use of a name, symbol, or label not because it represents an authentic reality, but because it is useful as a tool for power, legitimacy, or manipulation.

Islamic movements—most prominently the Muslim Brotherhood, founded in 1928—recognized that openly calling for the restoration of the Caliphate would provoke repression from the new nationalist regimes. Yet they also saw in the issue of Palestine a divine opportunity to reignite the passions of the ummah under the guise of resistance. By branding the fight for Palestine as a religious obligation—jihad against infidels who had desecrated sacred Islamic land—they could rally Muslims without directly challenging Arab nationalist governments. The Al-Aqsa Mosque was rebranded as the frontline of Islamic dignity itself. The emotional and theological power of Jerusalem, amplified by historical memory of Islamic conquests, was weaponized to reawaken religious fervor across populations being secularized from above. This allowed Islamic movements to galvanize mass support, recruit fighters, and preach militancy under the banner of "Palestinian," while in reality laying the groundwork for a broader Islamic revival—a theological project aimed at re-Islamizing a Muslim world that had been saturated with Western legal codes, secular education systems, and nationalist ideologies imposed to remold societies in the image of the West.

The Bolsheviks, seeking to undermine British and French dominance, attempted to export Marxism into the Arab world by framing anti-Zionism as part of the global struggle against imperialism. For the Soviet Union, Zionism was recast as a colonial enterprise, imposed on the Arab masses by Western capitalism. This narrative was formalized in Comintern resolutions of the 1920s and 1930s, which explicitly linked the "Palestine question" to the worldwide liberation of oppressed peoples. Soviet propaganda consistently depicted Jews in Palestine not as a people returning to their ancestral homeland but as agents of British imperialism. After 1948, the USSR entrenched this rhetoric further, supplying Arab regimes with weapons and saturating the region with ideological literature that cast Israel as nothing more than an outpost of Western exploitation. In doing so, the Soviets used "Palestine" as a convenient rallying cry through which Marxism could penetrate Arab societies under the guise of anti-colonial solidarity.

Arab dictators had their own incentives to inflate the Palestinian issue. Regimes that had failed to deliver prosperity or freedom discovered the political goldmine of externalizing failure. If Israel could be blamed for poverty, tyranny, military defeats, and stagnation, then corrupt elites could continue ruling with impunity. Israel became the scapegoat that allowed Arab rulers to survive. The key to sustaining that narrative was not merely the existence of Israel, but the perpetual misery of Palestinian refugees. Rather than resettling them, Arab governments deliberately kept Palestinians in camps, denying them citizenship, property rights, and economic integration. They were kept poor to remain politically useful. By contrast, Israel absorbed some 850,000 Jewish refugees expelled from Arab lands, granting them citizenship and integrating them into society.[34] No camps. No intergenerational victimhood. Palestinians were not victims of Israel, but of Arab regimes who weaponized them for political theater. The so-called "right of return" was never meant as a solution—it was a perpetual talking point, a tool to delay peace and sustain hatred.

No leader exemplified this nominal use of Palestine better than Egypt's Gamal Abdel Nasser. Initially, Nasser was willing to explore peace—even reaching out to Israel in 1956 through an American Quaker intermediary. But when his requests for Western arms were rejected, he turned to the Soviet Union and transformed himself into the icon of Arab anti-Zionism.[35] For Nasser, Palestine was not a humanitarian concern but a vehicle for unifying the Arab world under his brand of socialist nationalism. His political genius was in reframing defeat as heroism: even after the crushing loss of the Six-Day War in 1967, he retained support because he had "fought for Palestine." Results did not matter; appearances did. Other Arab leaders quickly learned the lesson: adopting Palestine as a cause was the surest way to suppress dissent at home while posturing as revolutionaries abroad.

While Nasser hijacked Palestine to construct a secular pan-Arab identity, his rival, King Faisal of Saudi Arabia, weaponized it in religious terms. Threatened by Nasser's republicanism and the appeal of Arab socialism, Faisal feared that pan-Arab nationalism would sweep away monarchies. To counter it, he turned to the very Islamic movements that Nasser had repressed. The Muslim Brotherhood, crushed in Egypt, found refuge and financing in Saudi Arabia. The decisive shift came after the Six-Day War. At the Khartoum Summit of 1967, Nasser arrived humiliated, militarily defeated, and economically desperate. Faisal, now ascendant and backed by oil wealth, held the leverage. In exchange for Saudi financial aid to rescue Egypt, Faisal demanded the release of imprisoned Muslim Brotherhood leaders.[36] Nasser, weakened and cornered, agreed. By freeing the Brotherhood, Faisal reintroduced a powerful Islamic current into Arab politics.

This was the turning point. With Saudi wealth behind them, Islamic movements flourished. Mosques, schools, media, and charities across the region preached a theologically charged version of anti-Zionism. Where Arab nationalism had failed, re-Islamization succeeded. It reshaped societies from the inside out. Secular modernist legacies of British and French rule were erased. Arab identity was no longer defined by language, law, or territory, but by allegiance to Islamic struggle. And Palestine became the vessel through which this ideological order was preached and enforced.

Even the Shi'a world, traditionally distant from Sunni causes, was swept into the current. After Iran's 1979 revolution, Ayatollah Khomeini declared the last Friday of Ramadan to be *Al-Quds Day*, making the "liberation of Jerusalem" a pillar of his foreign policy. Through proxies like Hezbollah, Iran embedded itself in the Palestinian cause—not because it loved Palestinians, but because it recognized that the road to Arab hearts was paved with anti-Zionism. Thus, Palestine became the single thread binding together otherwise irreconcilable ideologies: secular Arab nationalism, Sunni revivalism, Shi'a theocracy, and tribal monarchies—all converging in opposition to Israel.

HIJACKING JERUSALEM

The Islamic hijacking of the land of Israel did not begin in the 20th century, nor was it merely a reaction to Zionism or the modern state of Israel. Its roots reach deep into the earliest years of Islam's imperial expansion, when theological manipulations and political opportunism transformed Jerusalem into an ideological flashpoint. Long before the Palestinian cause was manufactured as a unifying symbol of Arab and Islamic grievance, the biblical homeland—specifically Jerusalem—had already been appropriated by Islamic rulers seeking legitimacy, power, and dominance within their fractured world.

The conquest of Jerusalem by the armies of the Rashidun Caliph ʿUmar ibn al-Khattab in 637 CE marked the first formal Islamic intrusion into the Jewish homeland. Yet the city held no inherent theological significance in early Islam. Muhammad initially directed his followers to pray toward Jerusalem not out of doctrinal conviction, but as a political maneuver to win favor with the Jewish tribes of Medina and to present himself as the continuation of their prophetic tradition. When those tribes rejected his claim to prophethood, he abruptly reversed course, shifting the qibla permanently to Mecca—a move that was both theological and political. Even the Qur'an's account of the Prophet's night journey (al-Isrāʾ wa-al-Miʿrāj) is vague, mentioning only "the farthest mosque" (al-Masjid al-Aqṣā) without geographical clarity and without naming Jerusalem. At the time of Muhammad's life, no mosque existed there. This ambiguity created fertile ground for later invention.

It was during the bloody civil war between ʿAbd al-Malik ibn Marwān and his rival ʿAbd Allāh ibn al-Zubayr, nearly fifty years after Muhammad's death, that the modern Islamic fixation on Jerusalem was born. Cut off from Mecca and Medina—both under ibn al-Zubayr's control—ʿAbd al-Malik faced a profound legitimacy crisis.

Pilgrimage to Mecca, the spiritual heart of Islam, was inaccessible to his subjects, undermining the symbolic core of his rule. His solution was as shrewd as it was radical: he redirected the religious imagination of Muslims toward Jerusalem. Around 691 CE, he ordered the construction of the Dome of the Rock on the Temple Mount—the very place where the Jewish Temple had once stood. By elevating Jerusalem as Islam's "third holiest site," he created a rival spiritual center that bound loyalty to his dynasty. The vague Qur'anic phrase "al-Masjid al-Aqṣā" was retroactively anchored to Jerusalem, and a flood of hadith and interpretations followed, tying the Prophet's night journey to the city and rewriting sacred geography.[37]

The result was devastatingly effective. Within a generation, devotion to Jerusalem had been cemented not through revelation but through political necessity. A sacred geography had been invented, and once invented, it could not be undone without existential crisis. The memory of the Jewish Temple was buried, and in its place a Muslim narrative took root, declaring Jerusalem to have always belonged to Islam. ʿAbd al-Malik did not have to fabricate this out of nothing—Islam's supersessionist theology already lent itself to the appropriation of Jewish and Christian symbols. He merely weaponized it to solve his political problem.

For centuries this myth lay dormant, only to reawaken with the rise of modern Zionism. As Jews began returning to their ancestral homeland in the late 19th century, the Islamic imagination revived its old claim with renewed intensity. Yet it was the establishment of the State of Israel in 1948—and especially Israel's capture of Jerusalem in the

Six-Day War of 1967—that reignited the second great hijacking of the city. The loss of the Temple Mount to Jewish sovereignty was not merely a military defeat but a theological crisis, striking at the core of centuries of Islamic appropriation. If Jews could reclaim the very ground Islam had declared its own, then Islam's claim of supremacy was exposed as fragile.

And so, the appropriation deepened. Al-Aqsa became the rallying cry of 20th-century Islamic movements. From Hamas in Gaza to Hezbollah in Lebanon, Jerusalem was invoked as the epicenter of grievance and jihad. Sermons thundered with accusations of Jews "defiling" al-Aqsa, even though Israel uniquely preserved Muslim access to the site. Facts mattered little—the myth was everything. Al-Aqsa was transformed into a symbol not only of lost sovereignty but of apocalyptic destiny. Both Sunni and Shi'a eschatologies invested Jerusalem with end-time significance: the Mahdi would arise, Jesus would return, and the final battle would be fought there against the Jews.

Thus the same city that 'Abd al-Malik once instrumentalized for dynastic survival has become the beating heart of a global ideology. Jerusalem's sanctification was not born of revelation, but of necessity—and in the 20th century, that necessity was reborn as propaganda, jihad, and eschatology.

A HISTORY OF DEFENSIVE CONFLICT

If the hijacking of Palestine was the foundational lie, then the portrayal of Israel as the aggressor is its most malignant offspring. To grasp the nature of this conflict, one must begin with a rarely asked but decisive question: *When did Israel initiate aggression?* The answer, stripped of propaganda and anchored in historical fact, is unequivocal: Israel never did. The modern State of Israel did not arise through conquest but through internationally sanctioned diplomacy and existential necessity.

In 1947, the United Nations passed Resolution 181, proposing the partition of the British Mandate into two states, one Jewish and one Arab. The Jewish leadership, despite painful compromises and grave security risks, accepted the plan. The Arab League categorically rejected it. On May 14, 1948, as David Ben-Gurion read Israel's Declaration of Independence, he appealed to the Arab population:

> "We appeal, in the very midst of the onslaught launched against us now for months, to the Arab inhabitants of the State of Israel to preserve peace and participate in the building of the State on the basis of full and equal citizenship and due representation in all its provisional and permanent institutions."[38]

The next day, five Arab armies—Egypt, Transjordan, Syria, Lebanon, and Iraq—invaded, vowing to annihilate the nascent state. Arab League Secretary-General Azzam Pasha promised a war of extermination. Israel, outnumbered and under-equipped, was forced into a war of survival. It did not seek war. It responded to it.

The 1948 war created two refugee populations, but only one was politically weaponized. Arab regimes deliberately prevented the resettlement of Palestinian refugees, trapping them in camps to be used as perpetual symbols of grievance. Syrian Prime Minister Khaled al-Azm admitted this years later in his memoirs (1972):

> "Since 1948, it is we who made them leave. We brought disaster upon Arab refugees, by bringing pressure upon them to leave Israel. We have rendered them dispossessed. Then we exploited them in executing crimes of murder, arson, and throwing bombs upon men, women, and children—all of this in the service of political purposes."[39]

At the same time, over 850,000 Jews were expelled from Arab countries—Iraq, Egypt, Syria, Yemen, Morocco, and others—forced to abandon homes, businesses, and centuries-old communities. Unlike the Palestinians, they were not left to rot in camps. Israel absorbed them, granted them citizenship, and built a future with them. Today their descendants make up the majority of Israel's Jewish population. They moved on. The Arab world did not.

The pattern of defensive wars repeated itself. In 1956, Gamal Abdel Nasser nationalized the Suez Canal and blockaded the Straits of Tiran—an act of war under international law. Israel, together with Britain and France, intervened to reopen the waterway. It was not conquest but survival. Israel withdrew after securing international guarantees, only to see them collapse a decade later. In 1967, Nasser again blockaded the Straits, expelled UN peacekeepers, massed troops on Israel's borders, and declared his intent to destroy the Jewish state. Jordan and Syria joined in a military pact. Facing annihilation, Israel struck first. In six days, it captured Gaza, Sinai, the West Bank, and the Golan Heights—defensive gains, not imperial acquisitions. Prime Minister Levi Eshkol immediately offered to return most of the land in exchange for peace. The Arab League answered with the Khartoum Resolution: *No peace. No recognition. No negotiations.*

In 1973, on Yom Kippur—the holiest day of the Jewish year—Egypt and Syria launched a surprise assault. Israel suffered devastating early losses but fought back to survive. Again, it had not started the war; it was ambushed while in prayer and fasting.

When direct wars failed, terrorism became the weapon. From the 1970s onward, the PLO and its affiliates waged a campaign of global terror: hijacking planes, bombing synagogues, massacring Israeli athletes at the Munich Olympics, and targeting civilians worldwide. Even when Israel signed peace with Egypt in 1978, returning the entire Sinai Peninsula—three times Israel's size—the broader Arab world's hostility persisted.

In 1982, Israel invaded Lebanon, not to conquer but to halt a decade of cross-border attacks from PLO strongholds. Southern Lebanon had become a launching pad for rockets and terror raids. The goal was security, not annexation. The operation expanded and grew messy, but its origin was unmistakably defensive.

The Oslo Accords of the 1990s seemed to offer a breakthrough. Israel recognized the PLO, allowed Yasser Arafat to return from exile, and granted the Palestinian Authority autonomy in major West Bank cities. Yet this unprecedented concession produced no peace. In 2000, after rejecting a peace proposal that offered nearly all of the

West Bank, Gaza, and shared sovereignty in Jerusalem, Arafat unleashed the Second Intifada. Suicide bombings, shootings, and terror attacks killed over 1,000 Israeli civilians.

In 2005, Israel withdrew unilaterally from Gaza, dismantling every settlement and removing every soldier. There was no occupation. Yet within two years, Hamas staged a bloody coup against the Palestinian Authority, seizing Gaza and turning it into a fortress of terror. Rocket fire on Israeli towns followed relentlessly. Israel responded not with conquest but with defense: targeting rocket launchers, terror tunnels, and military infrastructure.

This pattern culminated in its most horrific form on October 7, 2023. Hamas terrorists stormed across the border, massacring 1,400 Israelis—men, women, children, even infants—in the deadliest single day for Jews since the Holocaust. For Israel, survival now meant nothing less than the total dismantling of Hamas. Again, Israel did not start the war. It was forced into it.

From 1948 to 2023, one reality shines through: Israel never initiates. It responds. It defends. It survives. The aggressor, time and again, is not Israel but those who deny its very right to exist.

THE TWO-STATE SOLUTION

The two-state solution rests on a false diagnosis. It assumes the conflict is about borders when, in truth, it has always been about existence. Benjamin Netanyahu, often maligned in global media and by political opponents as an obstacle to peace, recognized this long before it became undeniable. As early as 1994, when Yitzhak Rabin was prepared to grant the Palestinians a state, Netanyahu warned of the danger: one does not hand sovereignty to a people whose ideology openly calls for your annihilation.

His concerns were not theoretical. A Palestinian state in the West Bank—the biblical heartland of Judea and Samaria—would leave Israel nine miles wide at its most vulnerable point. From those ridges, rockets could reach Tel Aviv, Jerusalem, and Ben-Gurion Airport in minutes. Geography alone makes such a withdrawal reckless. But geography is only half the problem. The moral dimension is equally clear. The Palestinians the world insists are "ready for statehood" have, time and again, demonstrated that they are not seeking peace beside Israel but Israel's destruction instead.

The record speaks for itself. In 2000, Prime Minister Ehud Barak offered Yasser Arafat nearly all of the West Bank, parts of East Jerusalem, and sovereignty over Gaza. Arafat walked away—not because the offer was inadequate, but because his mission was not to establish a state *beside* Israel, but to build one *instead of* Israel. In 2005, Ariel Sharon uprooted more than 8,000 Jews from Gaza, dismantled their communities, and handed the entire territory to Palestinian control. The world waited to see what Palestinians would create with this gift of autonomy. The answer was rockets. Gaza became a terror factory run by Hamas, funded with foreign aid, and transformed into a launching pad for jihad. When jihadist movements are given sovereignty, they do not build states—they build slaughterhouses.

Before 1967, there was no Israeli presence in Gaza or

the West Bank. Gaza was under Egyptian control; Jordan had annexed the West Bank and East Jerusalem.[40] Yet no Palestinian state was established. Why not? If the true goal was independence, why did no Arab government create one during those years? The answer is simple: because the issue was never statehood—it was sovereignty. And more precisely, Jewish sovereignty. What assurance, then, can Israel have that a return to the pre-1967 lines—borders that never once brought peace—would suddenly create stability? Why should Israel believe that handing over territory today would not repeat the Gaza catastrophe tomorrow?

Israel's history shows it is willing to trade land for peace—but only when peace is genuine. In 1979, it returned the entire Sinai Peninsula to Egypt—land three times Israel's size—after Anwar Sadat signed a peace treaty. Sadat paid with his life, assassinated by the Muslims Brotherhood who called peace with Israel treason. In 1994, King Hussein of Jordan faced similar denunciations when he signed his treaty. Even Syria, in the 1990s, nearly reached an agreement with Yitzhak Rabin for a return of the Golan Heights. The lesson is undeniable: when Arab leaders genuinely choose peace, Israel reciprocates. Land is negotiable. Existence is not.

The two-state solution did not collapse at Camp David, or at Oslo, or at Annapolis. It collapsed in the streets of Tel Aviv, in the buses torn apart by suicide bombers, in the kindergartens of Sderot shelled by rockets, and in the cafés of Jerusalem rocked by terror. It died in the chants of Hamas parades, in the textbooks that erase Israel from the map, in sermons that sanctify martyrdom. It died when Palestinians celebrated massacres as victories.

Statehood demands more than international sympathy. A two-state solution requires recognition of the other's right to exist. It requires responsibility, stability, and the abandonment of death-worship as a political creed. So long as Palestinian ideology exalts conquest over coexistence and martyrdom over life, Israel will do what any sovereign nation must: defend its people. Barriers, checkpoints, and military infrastructure are not instruments of colonial expansion. They are shields against annihilation.

The truth is simple: the two-state solution is not dormant—it is obsolete. It is eclipsed by an ideology that sees the very existence of Israel not as a partner for peace, but as a theological offense to be erased. Until that ideology changes, no border will be wide enough, and no concession deep enough, to buy peace.

THE THEOLOGICAL WAR AGAINST ISRAEL

The war against Israel is not a border dispute. It is not about settlements, checkpoints, or territory. It is a theological crusade rooted in an Islamic ideology that demands the eradication of Jewish sovereignty to restore a global caliphate. In this worldview, Israel's existence is not just inconvenient—it is an affront to Allah's will.

Hamas embodies this vision. In a leaked 2006 video, co-founder Mahmoud al-Zahhar declared: *"Our project is larger than Palestine. Palestine is like a toothpick, very small."*[41] His words strip away every illusion: Hamas does not fight for a Palestinian state but for a global Islamic order. For them, Palestine is merely the first battlefield, a stepping stone toward dismantling the system of nation-states and replacing it with a borderless caliphate governed by Sharia.

Hamas is not an anomaly but the Palestinian branch of the Muslim Brotherhood,[42] founded in Egypt in 1928 by Hassan al-Banna with the explicit mission of restoring Islamic supremacy worldwide. Al-Banna's writings outline the Brotherhood's creed: no recognition of national borders; the supremacy of Islam over all systems; infiltration through schools, charities, and institutions; political manipulation to capture governance; and, when conditions permit, armed jihad. Hamas, formed in 1987 during the First Intifada, is the Brotherhood's spear in Palestine. Its rockets and tunnels serve the same goal its parent organization set nearly a century ago: not statehood, but Islamization through war.

This ideology resonates far beyond Hamas. Across the Arab world, many Muslims see the 1916 Sykes-Picot Agreement as a Western plot to fracture the ummah. The modern nation-state is, in their view, a colonial fiction destined to collapse. In this theology, Arab weakness is not explained by poverty or corruption but by betrayal—by Muslim leaders who serve foreign powers instead of God, and by the persistence of Jewish sovereignty in the heart of Islamic land. That is why even Al-Azhar University—the so-called bastion of "moderate" Sunni Islam—repeatedly affirms that the war against Israel is not political but sacred. On October 7, 2023, as Hamas massacred Israeli civilians, Al-Azhar's Grand Imam Ahmed al-Tayeb praised them: *"Hamas has returned the soul to the Islamic ummah."*[43] This is not fringe rhetoric. Al-Azhar, revered as Sunni Islam's highest authority, has never categorically condemned jihad against Israel. On the contrary, in 2015 it issued a statement calling for global Islamic support for the "mujahideen"* in Jerusalem. Its scholars, sermons, and curricula consistently portray Israel as an "occupying enemy" and jihad for its destruction as "an obligation upon the ummah."

This is why the spectrum collapses. If the most authoritative "moderate" institution in Islam sanctifies violence against Jews, then there is no center ground. Hamas may fire the rockets, but Al-Azhar provides the scripture. One wages jihad with blood, the other with fatwas. Both converge on the same conclusion: the destruction of the Jewish state is not political—it is Islamic. This same institution produced Abdullah Azzam, mentor to Osama bin Laden, and Sayyid Qutb, whose *Milestones* became the manifesto of global jihad. Their ideological offspring—whether Hamas fighters in Gaza, Saraya al-Quds militias in Jenin, or al-Qaeda operatives in New York—drink from the same theological well.

The roots of this theology lie not in modern geopolitics but in the life of Muhammad himself. A hadith in *Sahih Muslim* states: *"The Last Hour will not come until the Muslims fight the Jews and the Muslims kill them, until the Jew hides behind a stone or a tree, and the stone or tree says: 'O Muslim, O servant of Allah, there is a Jew behind me; come and kill him.'"* This apocalyptic text casts the war against Jews as divine destiny, long before the state of Israel existed. The prece-

---

* **Mujahideen:** Arabic for "those who struggle." In Islamic usage, it refers to fighters engaged in *jihad*. In modern history, the term became widely known for the Afghan guerrillas who fought against the Soviet Union in the 1980s.

dent was set in Muhammad's lifetime: the massacre of the Banu Qurayza tribe in 627 CE, when 600–900 Jewish men and boys were executed,[44] and the 628 CE conquest of Khaybar, where Jews were enslaved and their lands seized. These are not rejected episodes in Islamic memory—they are celebrated. The chant "Khaybar, Khaybar, O Jews, Muhammad's army will return" still echoes in rallies across the Islamic world, a promise that history will be repeated.

Other hadiths sharpen this animus. In *Sunan Abu Dawud*, Muhammad declares: *"I will expel the Jews and Christians from the Arabian Peninsula and will not leave any but Muslims."*[45] In *Jami' at-Tirmidhi*, he instructs: *"If you meet a Jew or a Christian on the road, do not greet him with peace, but force him into the narrowest part of it."*[46] These sayings are treated as timeless injunctions. They ensure that hostility toward Jews is not a matter of politics but of creed.

Even Muhammad's own tactics serve as a model for today's jihadist methods. When the Quraysh plotted to assassinate him, he instructed his young cousin Ali—barely in his teens—to sleep in his bed as a decoy while he fled. Ali could have been killed, but Muhammad justified it by claiming Allah would protect him.[47] This precedent legitimizes the use of children as shields for the mission. It explains why Hamas hides rocket launchers in schools, mosques, and hospitals, and why they dare Israel to strike where civilians dwell. The precedent was set by the Prophet himself.

This is why the cry of *"Allahu Akbar"* unites Hamas, Saraya al-Quds, al-Qaeda, ISIS, Boko Haram, and lone-wolf terrorists in Europe. Their campaigns may differ in geography—massacring Yazidis in Iraq, slaughtering Christians in Nigeria, Islamizing Europe, or annihilating Israel—but their theology is the same. The war against Israel is not an isolated conflict. It is part of a seamless, global jihad, woven together by the same prophetic precedents, the same sacred texts, and the same conviction: that no sovereignty but Allah's may stand, least of all a Jewish one in the land once claimed by Islam.

ISRAEL'S MORAL DILEMMA

Imagine a trolley racing down a track. Five people are tied to the rails ahead. You can pull a lever to divert it, but on that track one person is tied down. Ethically, it is an impossible choice: allow five to die, or sacrifice one to save them. Most people, after agonizing, would pull the lever. Now imagine the one is your child, and the five are strangers. What would you do then?

This is the gut-wrenching moral trap Israel faces in Gaza—a trap engineered by Hamas, a jihadist movement that thrives on death and manipulates the world's conscience. On October 7, 2023, Hamas dragged more than 250 hostages into Gaza. From that moment forward, Hamas tied Israeli children to one side of the tracks and Palestinian civilians to the other. They embedded rocket launchers in schools, stashed weapons in hospitals, dug tunnels under UNRWA classrooms, and turned entire neighborhoods into human shields. Israel is forced to choose: act to protect its citizens at the risk of civilian casualties, or do nothing and allow Hamas terror to continue unchecked. Either way, Hamas ensures Israel is damned.

Hamas leaders make their strategy explicit. In 2018, Yahya Sinwar, then Hamas's Gaza chief, declared on Al-Aqsa TV: *"Our blood is our strength; martyrdom is our path to victory."* From October 2023 through July 2025, Hamas fired more than 15,000 rockets, almost all from densely populated areas. Residents who tried to flee reported being threatened at gunpoint by Hamas fighters to remain, guaranteeing civilian deaths for propaganda. Every dead Palestinian is weaponized: every grieving mother a headline, every Israeli airstrike a stage for condemnation.

And yet Israel labors to untie the rails. The IDF drops leaflets, sends text messages, and uses "roof-knocking" with non-lethal devices to warn civilians before strikes. Between October 2023 and July 2025, Israel delivered 1.8 million tons of food, medicine, and fuel into Gaza—even as Hamas siphoned off the aid for its fighters. Israeli strikes target rocket launchers, command centers, and tunnel networks, not civilians. But Hamas guarantees that civilians die by design. Imagine a father forced to choose between his child's life and strangers tied to the rails—knowing the strangers' own leaders bound them there. What nation would choose surrender?

Consider the contrast with the West Bank. From 2005 to 2023, more Israelis were killed by terrorists originating from the West Bank than from Gaza—through shootings, stabbings, and car-rammings. Yet Israel almost never bombed The West Bank from the air.[48] Why? Because there were no rocket barrages from those cities raining down on Tel Aviv or Ashkelon. Where there are no missiles, Israel sends in ground forces, risking its soldiers' lives to target militants door-to-door. Gaza is different. Gaza launches missiles, builds terror tunnels, and stocks weapons in apartment blocks. Israel responds to the weapons, not the population.

The moral chasm could not be clearer. When Baruch Goldstein, a Jewish extremist, massacred 29 Palestinians in Hebron's Cave of the Patriarchs in 1994, Israel recoiled in horror. Prime Minister Shimon Peres stood in the Knesset and denounced Goldstein as a *"disgusting, criminal traitor,"* comparing him to the Nazis. Goldstein was buried in disgrace, his movement outlawed, his followers marginalized. No schools named in his honor. Israel prosecuted its extremists and erased them from public life.

Contrast that with Gaza, where on October 7, 2023, Hamas's massacre of Israeli civilians was celebrated with gunfire in the streets, candy handed out to children, and chants of praise from mosque pulpits. Across much of the Islamic world, suicide bombers are lionized as martyrs. In Palestine, families are rewarded financially, and murderers of civilians are immortalized as heroes. Israel builds bomb shelters for its children. Hamas trains its children to become bombs.

This is Israel's moral dilemma. A democracy fighting for survival against an enemy that weaponizes its own civilians while glorifying the death of Israel's. It is not a contest between equal claims, but a struggle between a nation that clings to life and a movement that sanctifies death.

THE TWIN ENGINES OF ETERNAL JIHAD

To understand any modern conflict involving an Islamic entity, one must begin with a single axis: Caliphate or Wilaya. Every movement, every slogan, every act of violence emanates from one of these two doctrines, the twin engines of eternal jihad.

For Sunni Islam, the engine is the command to restore the *Caliphate*: a single, borderless Islamic state destined to encompass the entire world. The obligation to spread Islamic governance is embedded in Qur'an, Hadith, and centuries of jurisprudence, reinforced by legal consensus, and still preached today from pulpits across the Muslim world. This is why organizations like Hamas, al-Qaeda, ISIS, Boko Haram, and al-Shabaab all sound eerily alike once stripped of local context. Different theaters, same war. They are not nationalist movements. They are not indigenous liberation fronts. They are armies of the Caliphate. Their goal is not merely to reclaim land, but to impose sovereignty—Islamic sovereignty—over all lands.

But jihad never speaks its true name. It always cloaks itself. It calls itself *resistance*. It masquerades as an *anti-colonial struggle*. It borrows Western vocabulary—*freedom, dignity, self-determination*—only to hollow those words out and stuff them with theological warfare. This is how Hamas frames its cause. It does not parade openly under its charter, which calls for Israel's destruction, or the Muslims Brotherhood's charter, which calls for the global imposition of Sharia. Instead, it waves the flag of Palestine but prays for the banner of the Caliphate.

Shia Islam follows a different but equally totalizing

blueprint: *Wilayat al-Faqih*—the rule of the Islamic jurist. Developed most systematically by Ayatollah Khomeini, this doctrine merges spiritual and political authority under the guardianship of a Shia cleric until the return of the Mahdi. For the Mahdi to return, Shia eschatology demands that they secure the Hijaz—Mecca and Medina. Hence, Hezbollah in Lebanon, Hashd al-Shaabi in Iraq, and the Houthis in Yemen fight not merely for politics but for prophecy, aiming to build a corridor of Shia power from Tehran to the holy cities of Arabia. And like their Sunni counterparts, they veil their ambitions. Hezbollah claims to defend Lebanon. The Houthis wrap themselves in Yemeni nationalism. Hashd al-Shaabi swears allegiance to Iraq. Yet every one of them bows not to Beirut, Baghdad, or Sana'a—but to Qom.

Seventy-seven years of Arab-Israeli conflict—three full-scale wars, two intifadas, and countless military operations—have produced between 72,958 and 85,958 Arab deaths. Yet more than 50,000 of those, over two-thirds, have occurred since October 7, 2023, as the direct result of a war Hamas chose to launch. These numbers alone dismantle the propaganda of "genocide." Had Israel truly intended extermination, the toll would not have trickled slowly over decades; it would have been swift, massive, and undeniable. Instead, most of those killed have been armed militants, and the civilians who died were victims of Hamas's own strategy.

The war against Israel, then, is not a modern aberration. It is the most faithful continuation of Islamic history. From the fall of the Caliphate in 1924, every ideological current in the Muslim world has scrambled to restore it.

Pan-Arabism collapsed because it offered identity without theology, and it promised sovereignty without supremacy. What endured—what always endures—is the oldest impulse in Islamic political thought: to reclaim every inch of land once ruled by Islam and to wage eternal war until it is done.

Palestine became the vessel of that rage. A blank slate upon which Sunni Caliphal visions and Shia Wilayat ambitions could be projected. The same war that drove Umar ibn al-Khattab to conquer Jerusalem in 637, and Abd al-Malik to invent its sanctity in 691, fuels the war against Israel today. The slogans may change. The costumes may vary. But the engines of jihad remain the same: Caliphate and Wilaya, the twin doctrines that render peace not merely impossible, but heretical.

CHAPTER 3
WHY ISLAM IS INCOMPATIBLE WITH THE WEST

THE WAR OF STORIES

I am a Muslim, not by confession but by experience, having lived it for two decades. I am a Christian because I chose it and have walked its narrow road nearly as long. I am a Jew, not by blood, but because the Jewish imagination is etched into the contours of my thought. I am Jordanian by birth, Lebanese by becoming, and American by freedom. I have preached in mosques, baptized believers in rivers, and dwelled with monks in monasteries. I have watched pilgrims worship the blue-faced Murugan in Batu Caves, lit Shabbat candles, and joined the swelling choruses of prosperity gospel crowds in megachurches. From Cairo to Brussels, Istanbul to Paris, Dubai to New York—wherever I stood, and alongside whomever I stood—I saw one truth: we are all the products of a story.

A narrative is the lens through which we interpret reality, the architecture beneath our instincts. That story determines how we see ourselves and how we treat others. It decides whether we value life or cheapen it, whether we build societies anchored in dignity or in domination. It shapes whether our economies reward innovation or corruption, whether our legal systems pursue impartial justice or calcify into privilege. It governs how we respond to failure—whether we repent and reform, or entrench and implode. It teaches us to stand in courage or shrink in fear.

Yet while people are equal in their humanity, stories are not equal in their consequences. Some elevate, others enslave. Some teach us to love the stranger, others command us to kill him. Some cultivate conscience, reason, and restraint; others sanctify rage and conquest. The equality of persons is a moral truth. The equality of ideas is a dangerous fiction. Civilizations are shaped by beliefs, and beliefs—when codified into law, ritual, and education—generate radically different outcomes. The human heart may be universal in its longing, but the path it walks is carved by the story it believes. Not all stories are worthy of us. Not all stories build the world we want to live in. Some carry the seeds of progress; others carry the viruses of collapse.

If we are to measure the stories that shaped the modern world, then the feet of the immigrants cast the most honest vote. They vote with trudging across deserts, climbing into rafts, and crossing borders—for a chance to live under the shadow of a story that gave us Western civilization. It is the story that built cities where law is higher than power, where a poor man can sue the rich and win, where women walk unveiled and unafraid, where dissent is not treason but a right, and where the sacredness of the individual is not only encoded in constitutions but lived as reality.

Western civilization was created in the image of its God —the Judeo-Christian God—a sovereign Creator who is both just and merciful, who endows every human with inherent dignity (Genesis 1:27) and commands them to love their neighbor as themselves (Leviticus 19:18; Matthew 22:39). This creation was not instant but progressive, forged through centuries of trial and error: from the blood-soaked arenas of Rome to the cloistered scriptoria of medieval monasteries, from the Reformation's shattering of ecclesiastical tyranny to the Enlightenment's elevation of reason.

Yet the secular West, in its hubris, mistook culmination for cancellation—as if the story that shaped it was erased by the Age of Reason. But as historian Tom Holland argues in *Dominion: How the Christian Revolution Remade the World*, far from being supplanted, the biblical narrative made the Enlightenment possible: "To live in a Western country is to live in a society still utterly saturated by Christian concepts and assumptions."[1] The equality of all before the law, the freedom of conscience, the conviction that truth can be pursued through reason—these are not secular inventions but fruits of two millennia of theological wrestling, from Sinai's tablets to Golgotha's cross. The Enlightenment did not erase this story; it extended it, secularizing its language but not its soul. The West's moral architecture remains inseparable from the God who inspired it.

According to the United Nations, the number of international migrants reached 304 million in 2024, with the United States hosting 51 million—the highest in the world. Europe, by 2024, held nearly 94 million.[2] These migrations are indictments of failed narratives elsewhere and affirmations of Western civilization as the crown of human achievement. It is the place where women, once treated as property in nearly every culture, rose to lead nations and write laws. It is the place to which the oppressed of every continent turn their gaze, because the West became the only compass pointing toward justice. The abolition of slavery, the right to dissent, the dream of democracy, the cry of civil rights—all were forged in the furnace of Western self-correction.

In 2020, when rumors of election fraud swirled through the United States, I watched the world hold its breath. Not because they were American, but because America was their symbol of hope. If the light of justice flickered in the land that had carried the torch, what hope remained for the rest? In refugee camps, in prisons, in the homes of the silenced—all eyes turned to the West. For generations, it stood, though, at times, imperfectly, as the proof that power could be bound, that dignity could be defended, and that the story of man did not have to end in chains.

Western civilization is not merely a system; it is a sanctuary. Its laws, values, and moral architecture have sheltered dissidents, heretics, dreamers, reformers, and exiles. It alone dares to write its sins into its history books and teach its children never to repeat them. That is what makes it different. That is so much of what makes it worth defending.

THE HOLLOW THRONE

In March 2024, Richard Dawkins, the high priest of New Atheism, stood before the twilight of his own legacy and declared himself a "cultural Christian." This was no conversion, no Damascus-road epiphany. The man who authored *The God Delusion*, who for decades wielded his pen against the faith of his fathers, did not bow to Christ. Instead, he confessed that the West—his West—the civilization that cradled his reason and sheltered his dissent, was forged in the crucible of the Christian story, the very story he had spent his career dismantling.

In an LBC radio interview,[3] Dawkins lamented that London's Oxford Street displayed Ramadan lights instead of Easter decorations. "I do think we are culturally a Christian country," he admitted. "I love hymns and Christmas carols, and I sort of feel at home in the Christian ethos." He went further, declaring he would choose Christianity over Islam "every single time," citing Islam's "active hostility" to women and gays rooted not in culture but in its texts, the Qur'an and Hadith. This was not nostalgia for Christmas carols or cathedral choirs; it was recognition of a deeper truth: the story that shaped the West was under siege. Dawkins, the atheist who dismisses faith as delusion, saw that the vacuum he helped create was not neutral —it was being filled by a rival narrative, one that for fourteen centuries has carried a record of subjugation, intolerance, and theological absolutism. Historian Tom Holland observed the irony: Dawkins was "sitting on the branch he's been sawing through and gazing nervously at the ground far below,"[4] realizing that secularism had not liberated the West but disarmed it before an uncompromising creed.

In the twentieth century, secular humanists sought to dethrone the Judeo-Christian God, enthroning human reason as the sole architect of liberty, equality, and justice. They imagined that man could inherit the cathedral of Western morality without its cornerstone, as though the *imago Dei* could be severed from its sacred roots and still bear fruit. But by cutting the root, they hollowed the tree. They forgot what Friedrich Nietzsche, the prophet of nihilism, warned in *Twilight of the Idols*:

> "When one gives up the Christian faith, one pulls the right to Christian morality out from under one's feet... Christianity is a system, a whole view of things thought out together. By breaking one main concept out of it—the faith in God—one breaks the whole: nothing necessary remains in one's hands."[5]

You cannot hijack the West's story, recast its hero from God to frail, fallible man, and expect its pillars of liberty, justice, and dignity to stand unshaken. By exiling its divine preserver, secularism created a yawning void—a throne left empty. And history teaches that empty thrones are never left vacant for long.

VESSELS OF THE STORY

A civilization's story is not its geography; it is its people. Borders can be redrawn, cities renamed, empires rise and fall, but the identity of a civilization lives in the collective imagination of its people. Land is inert. Soil has no memory, no loyalty, no conviction. It does not weep when tyranny takes hold nor rejoice when liberty flourishes. It is the people who animate a civilization, encoding its story in rituals, laws, customs, and sacrifices. They transmit it through language, education, tradition, and the resolve to believe that their way of life is worth preserving.

The Jews understood this. Exiled for two millennia, they preserved their civilization not through territory, but through Torah, Sabbath, and memory. While empires devoured one another, the Jewish story endured them all. In 1948, when the State of Israel was reborn, it was not the soil that called them back, but the story they had never stopped telling. They did not return to find their civilization; they carried it with them. Likewise, the early Christians possessed no territory, commanded no armies, and wielded no political power. Yet their story—the gospel of a crucified and risen God—spread from the alleys of Jerusalem to the heart of imperial Rome. It toppled idols, redefined virtue, and reshaped the values of Western civilization without conquering a single square mile. Their faith, carried by martyrs and missionaries, transformed the very Roman empire that sought to erase them.

If the people change their story, the civilization changes with them, regardless of the land. Stories live or die in the hearts of those who carry them. And if a rival story gains ground—whether by demographic replacement, ideological indoctrination, or cultural capitulation—the civilization that once stood proud begins to erode from within. The monuments may still stand, the flag may still wave, the anthem may still play, but the soul has shifted. The land remains, but its meaning has been rewritten. Civilizations are not inherited like property; they are inherited like fire: they must be tended, guarded, and passed with reverence. Forget this, and geography will not save you. History is full of lands where people abandoned their story and became strangers in their own civilization. The West will not be saved by its landscapes. It will be saved—if at all—by a people willing to remember, defend, and live the story that made it worth fleeing to in the first place.

If the West forgets its story, it will lose its institutions. If it invites a rival story into its bloodstream—whether through migration, ideological surrender, or guilt-ridden self-negation—it will not remain the West.

WHAT IS INCOMPATIBILITY?

Incompatibility is the irreconcilable conflict between two narratives that claim different but mutually exclusive realities. Both cannot be true at the same time. It is not a clash of opinions, resolvable by debate or compromise, but a battle over the deepest questions of existence. As Samuel Huntington wrote in *The Clash of Civilizations*, "Conflicts between civilizations are the greatest conflicts because they arise from differing assumptions about the nature of reality and the ultimate values of human life."[6] When one story insists that every individual bears inherent dignity, worthy of liberty and equality before the law, while another declares that worth comes only through submission to a singular authority, there is no middle ground. These are not policies to negotiate; they are ontologies at war.

Over the past two decades, European nations poured

billions into integration programs for Muslims aimed at bridging cultural divides. Germany alone spent nearly €1.4 billion on integration courses between 2005 and 2013, and another €2.1 billion in 2016. Yet the results remain dismal. By 2012, less than 57% of participants passed the minimum B1-level German test, with completion rates hovering at barely half and dropout rates reaching 57%.[7] In the Netherlands, despite mandatory civic integration exams, as of 2016 nearly 90% of required participants had failed to pass or complete the program. Migrants are offered schools, courts, language programs, and democratic systems, but without the moral story that gives these institutions meaning. They are handed the shell of Western civilization without the inner code that animates it.

The greatest misconception about incompatibility is that it is merely cultural, a matter of food, dress, or custom, solvable through dialogue and education. But narratives are not accessories; they are blueprints for civilization. When the Magna Carta (1215) declared that no man is above the law, it was not a cultural quirk but a theological revolution rooted in the Judeo-Christian ethic of accountability.

Another misconception is that incompatibility can be ignored—that rival narratives can coexist indefinitely under the umbrella of tolerance. The West, in its generosity, embraced this illusion, believing its openness could hold all stories without cost. But pluralism is not universal. It is a fragile achievement, born of the Judeo-Christian belief that truth can withstand scrutiny and conscience must be free. Pluralism survives only when all parties agree to its rules. When a narrative enters that rejects pluralism itself—demanding exclusive allegiance, silencing dissent, or enforcing its moral order by law—tolerance becomes the West's Achilles' heel.

A final misconception is that incompatibility is abstract, a philosophical debate with no real-world stakes. But it is as tangible as the millions of migrants in 2024 who fled failed narratives for the West's promise of freedom; as concrete as the courts that uphold or deny rights; as visceral as the fear of a dissident when truth itself becomes a crime. Incompatibility is measured in the institutions it builds or destroys, in the lives it elevates or crushes.

When two stories claim the same soul, one must yield. A society cannot simultaneously defend freedom of speech and criminalize blasphemy, cannot champion gender equality while enforcing patriarchal hierarchies. One story will dominate the institutions, rewrite the laws, and redefine the future.

In this war of stories, confidence is king. A civilization uncertain of its own narrative, apologizing for its heritage, is already in decline. The West forgot the source of its greatness. It began treating its moral architecture as a human invention rather than an inherited truth. It replaced transcendent authority with procedural consensus. Rights became negotiable. When the sacred becomes a social construct, confidence collapses. A civilization that doubts its legitimacy begins to cede ground. That is what we see today: universities unable to define truth, courts reinventing rights with every decade, governments unsure of their authority to defend borders, societies debating the definition of "woman" while tolerating ideologies openly hostile to her existence. Meanwhile, rival systems advance with unshakable certainty. They are not here to integrate. They are here to replace. And they are winning.

Everything laid out thus far is not a eulogy but a diagnosis. It maps the fractures in the West's foundations, the dilution of its moral confidence, the slow replacement of its narrative with one foreign and hostile to it. Diagnosis, however, is only the beginning. The question is: can it be reversed? Reversal is not nostalgia—it is not a return to the past, but a recovery of the principles that built the West in the first place: the eternal architecture of its story. It demands courageous leadership, cultural reformation, theological clarity, and a population willing to reject the poison of relativism. The rival narrative does not wait. It advances while the West hesitates. That is why defense is no longer enough. Offense is required.

And offense does not mean violence. It means intellectual warfare, cultural clarity, strategic deconstruction of the rival story. It means exposing its roots, its incompatibilities, its anthropology that collapses the individual into the collective, its epistemology that shuts down scrutiny, its theology that rejects coexistence. This is not aggression. It is self-preservation.

HOW ISLAM CODES MORALITY

In the Judeo-Christian tradition, moral truth is rooted in God's character but discovered through a harmony of revelation, natural law, reason, and conscience. Scripture is central, but not isolated. Truth emerges from dialogue with the divine, not blind decree. Jacob wrestled with God and became Israel—*the one who wrestles*. That act of contending with the sacred was not rebellion but relationship. Western civilization itself was born out of this struggle: a barbaric and tribal world became civilized not by silencing doubt but by engaging it. It questioned, reasoned, philosophized, and in that long wrestling match between faith and reason, it forged the moral foundations of the West.

What made this possible was the Judeo-Christian conviction that man himself is sacred—made in the image of God, endowed with reason, conscience, and moral agency. These faculties were not rivals to revelation but part of it. The sacred was revealed in Scripture, yes, but also in creation, in logic, in the inner voice of conscience. In this worldview, texts became sacred precisely because they resonated with these faculties and illuminated the human soul. When passages appeared to contradict reason or conscience, they were debated, wrestled with, reinterpreted—and sometimes even rejected or re-framed. The sacred was not authoritarian; it was relational. This is why the West could develop moral philosophy, scientific inquiry, and democratic governance without severing itself from faith.

Islam leaves no such space. The Muslim story is confined to a single text—the Qur'an—and a single life—the Prophet Muhammad. The Qur'an is not to be interrogated by reason or conscience but obeyed. Surah 33:36 is explicit: *"It is not for a believing man or a believing woman, when Allah and His Messenger have decided a matter, to have any choice in their affair."* In Islam, the mind must bow. Reason is not a partner in revelation but a threat to it. If reason contradicts the Qur'an, reason must submit. If conscience recoils from a command, conscience must be silenced. The very name "Islam" means submission. The believer's role is not to wrestle, but to obey. Virtue is not measured by thoughtfulness or moral struggle, but by conformity. The life of Muhammad—ordering assassinations, taking child brides, distributing female captives as spoils of war—becomes the unquestionable template for human conduct, sacralized not as history but as timeless righteousness.

The consequences are profound. When moral authority derives solely from text, and that text has only one authoritative interpreter—the life of Muhammad—moral evolution becomes impossible. There can be no Aquinas to explore natural law, no Kierkegaard to wrestle with faith, no Kant, Locke, or Rousseau. There is no Enlightenment, because there is no oxygen to sustain one. Morality in Islam is not internal conviction but external decree. It is legalism, total and exhaustive. Islamic jurisprudence (*fiqh*) classifies every human act into five categories: obligatory, recommended, permissible, discouraged, and forbidden. Nothing escapes regulation—from how to wash before prayer, to whether one may greet a non-Muslim first, to whether a woman may raise her voice in public. Life is reduced to a labyrinth of divine rulings, and the supreme virtue is not compassion, wisdom, or justice—but obedience.

This framework infantilizes the believer, leaving him in permanent dependence on jurists to parse divine law. Conscience is rendered irrelevant. To follow conscience against the text is not courage but apostasy. The very category of conscience, as the West understands it, is absent. What matters is not the moral weight of an act but its correspondence to command. If divinely sanctioned, even cruelty is righteous. If forbidden, even compassion is sin.

And this is not theoretical—it defines Islamic societies. Schools, courts, mosques, and families are shaped by this ethic of obedience. The West grew by challenging its sacred texts—asking whether slavery, patriarchy, or persecution could be squared with their deeper spirit. Islam forbids the question. Its power lies in fidelity to the past, not transformation of it.

Consider the words of Sheikh Abu Ishaq al-Huwaini, among the most influential scholars of the 21st century. Speaking before an audience of jurists, he said that the Muslim world's economic decline was due to its abandonment of jihad.[8] He argued that Islam's prosperity had historically flowed from jihad itself—from war spoils, slaves, and captives that enriched the ummah. His point was not marginal but mainstream: that revival requires not reform, but restoration—resurrecting practices the modern conscience would call barbaric, yet which remain sanctified by the text.

In Islam, the past is not to be surpassed but reimposed. Justice is not an aspiration but a memory. And prosperity is not a goal of progress but a prize of conquest. This is how Islam codes morality.

SANCTIFICATION OF VIOLENCE

As I write these lines, harrowing videos and photos are emerging from southern Syria, where Muslim jihadists are massacring members of the Druze community whose only "crime" is demanding autonomy under a regime now led by a former ISIS commander. Their fear is the logical response of a people who have endured centuries of persecution under Islamic rule—part of a broader pattern in which religious and ethnic minorities across the Islamic world have been systematically marginalized, brutalized, and silenced since the earliest days of Islam.

The brutality on display—beheadings, mutilated corpses, rape, slavery—is not unique to Islamic civilization. History is replete with human cruelty. But what sets Islamic violence apart is not its scale or its methods, nor even the fact that it is unfolding in the 21st century. What makes it categorically different is that it is sacred. It is sacralized bloodshed—violence performed not in spite of faith, but because of it; commanded by revelation, justified by the prophetic model, and glorified as worship. We all have the potential for evil. But a Christian who commits murder is violating his faith. A Muslim who kills an apostate is fulfilling his. A Buddhist who wages war contradicts the teachings of his religion. A jihadist who slaughters unbelievers is doing precisely what his religion commands.

The easiest way to demonstrate how Islam constitutionalized violence would be to overwhelm you with raw data: the Qur'anic verses commanding the killing of nonbelievers (9:5); the beheadings (47:4); the threats of terror from Allah (9:14); the divine calls urging Muhammad to rally the believers to slaughter their enemies in exchange for paradise (8:65). I could list every verse glorifying jihad as the straightest path to heaven, and every promise that fighters who spill blood in Allah's name will be rewarded with the choicest place in Jannah (3:169–170). I could explain the doctrine of *naskh* (abrogation, 2:106) in Islamic jurisprudence and show how the verses quoted by apologists to claim Islam's "tolerance" were simply earlier revelations—later canceled once Muhammad's political power shifted. In Mecca, when he was weak, the Qur'an reflected a meek tone (109:1–6). In Medina, when he became a warlord, the tone hardened (9:28). I could walk you through the Sunnah, the sayings and actions of Muhammad, narrations that record the assassinations of poets, the killing of women, elders, tribes, caravans, even children; the 86 military campaigns he led or authorized. I could zoom out to 1,400 years of history and recount the 350 million-plus deaths directly resulting from jihad—the imperial conquests from Spain to India, the razing of Christian, Zoroastrian, Hindu, and Buddhist civilizations. I could cite the fact that over 96% of all globally designated terrorist organizations today are Islamic, or the more than 60,000 jihadist terrorist attacks carried out in 70 countries over the last 25 years.[9] I could dismantle the narrative that Islam is "open to interpretation" by showing that the Prophet's life—the *uswa hasana*, the "perfect example"—is the only valid lens for understanding the Qur'an, meaning that the ideal Muslim is not a philosopher, reformer, or peaceful neighbor, but a man who wages war, kills dissenters, enslaves women, and demands absolute allegiance.

But I will not do that here. Entire libraries have already cataloged these facts. What I want to show instead is more important: not simply how Islam *permits* or *commands* violence, but how it *sanctifies* it in the Muslim imagination —how brutality is beautified by the sacred text, normalized by Muhammad's example, and exalted through the mythologizing of Islamic conquests. Islam does not merely allow violence. It consecrates it.

This is why Islamic apologists labor to romanticize violent scripture. They wrap jihad in mysticism, reinterpret beheadings as metaphors, and elevate the calls to kill unbelievers into philosophical riddles. They insist the Qur'an is misunderstood, that the Prophet's sword was reluctant, that violence was conditional, defensive, or historical. But by this stage, the problem is not what the texts contain or how they might be reinterpreted. The deeper problem is how those texts function in the imagination of the believer.

When the medieval Catholic Church burned heretics, it was not obeying scripture. No Gospel verse commands the execution of dissenters or the torture of witches. What the Church possessed was not a violent text but a violent authority. It claimed institutional sanctity. It claimed to hold the keys to salvation. And when people believe eternal destiny hinges on obedience to an institution, that institution has absolute power. It does not need divine command to kill. It only needs heretics to threaten its authority, and believers desperate enough to defend it. This is how violence becomes sanctified—not through revelation, but through necessity. The killing of heretics was seen not as cruelty but as devotion. Burning someone at the stake was not betrayal of conscience but an act of faith in service of the Savior. When eternal reward is at stake, there is no moral cost too high. Loyalty replaces compassion as the measure of righteousness.

In such a framework, violence is no longer evil. It is

repurposed. It becomes a means to survive, to obey, to be cleansed. And this mechanism does not even require religion. It only requires an ideology that offers redemption—religious or secular.

Consider Adolf Eichmann, the Nazi bureaucrat who orchestrated the Holocaust's logistics. He was not a sadist or a deranged monster. When Holocaust survivor Yehiel Dinur collapsed at Eichmann's trial in 1962, he later explained: "It was not the memories that made me collapse. It was the realization that Eichmann was not a demon. He was an ordinary man." Eichmann was not psychopathic. He was a functionary. A man obeying orders in service of a cause greater than himself. The salvation of the Aryan race had been sacralized by the Third Reich. Eichmann's violence was not recreational. It was devotional. The Reich was his savior. Its utopian vision required his actions.

This is why Islamic terrorists blow themselves up. Not because they are insane, but because, like Eichmann, they have been given a theological structure in which violence is the path to transcendence. ISIS, al-Qaeda, Hamas—they do not teach their followers to hate for hate's sake. They teach that martyrdom is the highest calling, that killing unbelievers, Jews, and apostates is a ticket to paradise. The suicide bomber does not see women and children. He sees the straight road to heaven.

All powerful institutions need customers. The more desperate the customers, the greater the control. The medieval Catholic Church sold salvation through indulgences to souls terrified of hell. At that moment, the Church behaved no differently than any tyrannical regime preying on desperation. When the Protestant Reformation proclaimed that salvation was free—*sola fide*—it shattered the Church's monopoly. What followed was not only a theological revolt but an economic one, as a market of souls collapsed. The moment salvation was unchained from institutional control, the authority of the institution began to crumble. Power built on human desperation can endure for centuries, but once the soul no longer needs a gatekeeper, the gates themselves begin to fall.

THE COLLAPSE OF CONSCIENCE

At the core of the Islamic moral architecture lies a principle: *"Whatever is not explicitly prohibited by the text is permitted"* (mā lam yurd al-nass bi-taḥrīmihi fahuwa mubāḥ). This axiom does more than establish legal boundaries—it replaces moral reasoning. It reshapes the very moral psychology of the Muslim believer. Under this schema, anything not clearly forbidden by Allah or His Messenger is, by default, permissible.

An action is good not because it is intrinsically just, but because it has been commanded by Allah or modeled by Muhammad.

Asma bint Marwan was a poetess in Medina who criticized Muhammad. The Prophet is reported to have said: *"Who will rid me of the daughter of Marwan?"* Umayr bin Adiy, a companion from her own clan, volunteered. That night, while she slept with her infant in her arms, he crept into her home and murdered her in her bed. But as he left, Umayr felt the weight of his act. He questioned whether it was right. When he reported back to Muhammad, he asked directly if he bore guilt for what he had done. Muhammad replied: *"No two goats will butt their heads about her."* In other words, her death was not only justified but insignificant. He then commended Umayr, saying, *"You have helped Allah and His Messenger."*[10] The companion's momentary doubt—the flicker of conscience—was extinguished by prophetic sanction.

Islam, therefore, erases the foundations of natural law: the philosophical notion, affirmed across civilizations, that certain moral truths are inscribed in the human heart and accessible through reason and conscience. In Islam, the will of Allah overrides all. If He commands you to behead your father, as Abu Ubayda ibn al-Jarrah did at the Battle of Badr, then that act ceases to be a tragedy;[11] it becomes piety. Islam did not refine conscience—it replaced it. And in its place it installed a mechanical ethic of obedience. When moral value is confined to what has been textually prescribed, the entire ethical landscape warps. Instead of cultivating character, the believer is trained to comply.

In Islam, moral formation is not oriented toward compassion, justice, or the defense of the vulnerable. It is overwhelmingly directed toward the control of the body—above all, the female body. A man's righteousness is judged less by how he treats the poor or defends the weak, than by how rigorously he guards the "modesty" of his women. Covering a woman's hair, in this framework, becomes more urgent than feeding the hungry. Segregating her in schools becomes more important than defending the oppressed. Her visibility in public becomes more threatening than government corruption. The result is a saturation of the Muslim mind with ritual and sexual anxiety.

Entire sections of Islamic legal manuals are devoted to menstruation, emissions, intercourse, ablution, and the precise parameters of halal and haram in sexual relations. The believer's attention is redirected away from inner virtue toward external compliance. Conscience is not sharpened; it is drowned. And this saturation has consequences. It reroutes the moral energy of the entire community. Islamic societies do not produce widespread movements for abolition, civil rights, or philosophical reflection. They produce regimes of gender policing, modesty enforcement, and religious surveillance. Because the moral focus has shifted: righteousness is measured by sexual discipline, not justice. And sexual discipline itself is defined not by consent or dignity, but by the mechanical fulfillment of command.

THE PSYCHOLOGY OF TERROR AND LUST

In the moral imagination of Islam, tarheeb (threat) and targheeb (enticement) are the bedrock of moral instruction.[12] The Qur'an governs behavior by manipulating two primal forces: fear and desire. Tarheeb is the threat of hell, torture, burning flesh, and divine wrath. Targheeb is the promise of paradise, an eternal pleasure dome filled with sensual reward, gardens, rivers, gold, and virgins. Together, they form a total system of control.

I remember vividly how, as a child, I absorbed this psychological conditioning. I was taught that I was closest to God not when I felt peace, but when I felt terror. The more I trembled before His wrath, the more pious I believed I was. My favorite chapter to recite alone was

Surah Qaf. I still remember the chill I felt reading, "We are closer to him than his jugular vein," and "The Fire says: Are there any more to come?" The chapter painted hell in vivid, concrete images: bodies dragged by chains, scorching flames, angels of torment with no mercy in their eyes. But the fear was never alone. Right beside it, woven into the same passages or adjoining ones, came the dangling carrot of paradise. Not a paradise of moral union with God or spiritual fulfillment, but of raw, unrestrained sensuality. Rivers of wine, honey, and milk. Robes of silk. Thrones of gold. Virgin wives untouched by man or jinn. The Qur'an makes this imagery explicit in Surahs 44, 52, 55, 56, and 76. In Surah 78:33, the righteous are promised "kawa'ib atraaba", virgins with full, swelling breasts, matched in age. In Surah 76, they are waited upon by wildan (eternal youth) bearing goblets of wine, their skin described as "clear like crystal." Even the sensual descriptions of paradise's food and fabric are exaggerated to seduce the imagination.

As a boy, this blend of terror and lust shaped my brain. It shaped my emotional world. God was to be feared, not loved. Obedience was extracted not through moral admiration but through dread. And my vision of reward was carnal, not spiritual. I never once imagined paradise as the presence of the divine. I imagined it as relief from fear and indulgence of desire.

This psychological formation is systemic. The Qur'an employs tarheeb and targheeb in tandem as a behavioral mechanism. In Surah 4:56: "Those who disbelieve in Our revelations, We shall roast them in Fire. Whenever their skins are burned away, We shall replace them with new skins so they may taste the torment again." And in Surah 78:31–33, just a few verses later: "Indeed, for the righteous is triumph, gardens and grapevines, and full-breasted companions of equal age, and a cup overflowing." This sequencing is pedagogical strategy. One verse crushes the soul with fear. The next seduces the flesh with pleasure. It is the perfect feedback loop for psychological compliance. This characteristic of Islam is not a matter of opinion, Allah Himself affirms it in Surah As-Sajda, verses 13 to 16:

> "And if We had willed, We could have given every soul its guidance, but the word from Me will come into effect [that] "I will surely fill Hell with jinn and people all together. So taste [punishment] because you forgot the meeting of this, your Day; indeed, We have [accordingly] forgotten you. And taste the punishment of eternity for what you used to do."

This moral psychology aligns with Lawrence Kohlberg's stages of moral development,[13] a framework developed to understand how people evolve in their ethical reasoning. According to Kohlberg, the lowest stage of moral development, Stage One, is the "Obedience and Punishment Orientation," where actions are judged purely by their consequences. A child in this stage believes something is wrong because it leads to punishment, not because it violates a principle. The next stage, Stage Two, is the "Self-Interest Orientation," where right and wrong are measured by personal gain: "What's in it for me?" Islamic moral formation, as shaped by tarheeb and targheeb, is engineered to keep believers permanently trapped in these earliest stages. Do good to avoid hell. Do more to get the houris. Fear punishment. Desire pleasure. No internalization of principle. No development of conscience. No ascent beyond reward and threat. And this has consequences far beyond individual psychology, it explains the collective moral stagnation of Islamic societies. In a community shaped by this framework: A man does not avoid injustice because it is wrong. He avoids it because he fears divine retaliation. A woman does not dress modestly because of self-respect or social virtue. She covers because the hadith says that her hair will drag her to hellfire and bring down the community with her. Children are not taught to love the good, but to fear hell and crave paradise. This infantilizes the moral consciousness. It freezes entire generations in pre-conventional morality, unable to ascend into principled reasoning. It creates believers who do not question violence, because violence has been made divine. Believers who do not protest injustice, because conscience is untrained. And believers who cannot separate righteousness from reward.

Stages of Moral Development

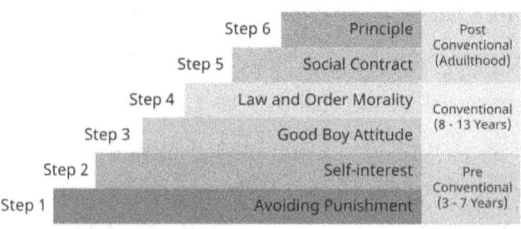

CLASH OF HORIZONS

Cognitive dissonance arises when a person holds two or more conflicting beliefs, values, or attitudes simultaneously. It is the internal tension between what one believes and what one observes, between doctrine and experience. Islam, by design, induces this dissonance in the modern Muslim mind. Take, for instance, the Qur'anic view of Jews and Christians. Surah Al-Ma'idah 5:51 commands: "O you who believe! Do not take the Jews and the Christians as allies. They are allies of each other. And whoever is an ally to them among you, then indeed, he is one of them." Surah Al-Tawbah 9:30 goes further: "The Jews say, 'Ezra is the son of Allah,' and the Christians say, 'The Messiah is the son of Allah.' ... May Allah destroy them; how deluded they are."

Yet the Muslim today often lives in secular societies, surrounded by Jews and Christians who show kindness, fairness, and goodwill. This generates dissonance. The horizon of Qur'anic command meets the horizon of reality. The non-Muslim who is painted as a cursed enemy appears in life as a generous friend. The Muslim, internally bound by dogma, is externally confronted by contradiction. The dissonance becomes intolerable. And because the Qur'an has no mechanism for revising itself, reality must be reinterpreted, not the text.

This is why facts don't matter. When the Arab-Israeli conflict is discussed, the empirical record—Arab rejections of peace, Israeli concessions, Jewish historical ties to the land—is irrelevant to the committed Muslim mind. It clashes with a horizon already constructed. In this horizon,

Jews are not a people with legitimate history, they are the cursed enemy of Allah. But this isn't just about Jews or Christians. The dissonance permeates all dimensions of life. The concept of authority, for example, is shaped by the Islamic view of God as an absolute, unchallengeable sovereign. In Islamic theology, God is not a relational father figure but an authoritarian master. Consequently, political authority is also expected to mirror that divine absolutism. This explains the difficulty Muslims have in creating democratic regimes, or fully integrating into secular democracies, where power is distributed, accountability is institutionalized, and the rule of law stands above religious mandate. These values contradict the horizon formed by Islam.

This clash between internal dogma and external reality also explains how terrorists are made. Imagine believing, without a shadow of a doubt, that God despises those who don't follow your religion. That He has commanded you to convert them, subjugate them, or kill them. But you are not violent. You want to live in peace. You benefit from secular society. You have non-Muslim friends. You enjoy their freedoms. You admire their culture. Yet every day, you recite prayers reminding you that those who go astray, Jews and Christians, are cursed. You begin to feel it. The guilt. The contradiction. You are not living your faith fully. The "true believers" tell you you're lukewarm. And they're right. You believe the text, but not enough to obey it. You're not killing infidels. You're not fighting jihad. You're coexisting, and you know that's not what your religion demands.

So, what do you do? You compensate. You cheer for those who do what you can't. You praise the mujahideen.

You justify terrorism. Or you say nothing. Silence is easier. You become the quiet apologist, the passive observer. The contradictions pile up. The dissonance eats at you. And then, some snap. Since 2001, over 60,000 Muslims have committed or attempted acts of terrorism. These are not just lunatics or radicals. Many are ordinary people who finally gave in to the logic of their beliefs. They could no longer bear the tension between the text and the world. So, they surrendered to jihad. They picked up the knife, the gun, the suicide vest—because they could no longer live in contradiction. They chose death over doubt. They wanted to align their lives with their beliefs. To stop living a lie. The horizon they inherited was not built for coexistence. It was built for conquest. And when that horizon meets the pluralism, secularism, and tolerance of modern life, it doesn't adjust. It collides.

LOSS AVERSION

A field study conducted by economist Colin Camerer in the late 1990s,[14] examined the real-world work patterns of New York City taxi drivers who rented their cabs by the day and kept their fares. The rational economic model predicted that drivers would work longer hours on busy days, such as when it rained or during holidays, because demand and profits were higher. Yet the data revealed the opposite. Most drivers quit early on good days and worked longer on slow days. Why? Because they weren't maximizing income, they were trying to meet a mental earnings target, typically around $100–$130 per day. Once they hit that number, they stopped, regardless of how favorable the conditions were. This behavior, though irrational from a purely economic standpoint, made perfect psychological sense. It illustrated what Daniel Kahneman and Amos Tversky called *loss aversion*:[15] the tendency for people to fear losses more than they value gains. Drivers weren't striving to earn more, they were trying not to earn less than their internal benchmark. They were motivated not by growth, but by the anxiety of underperformance. And this pattern—hitting the minimum and stopping—is precisely what any fear-based system tends to produce, whether in the workforce or in religion.

In Islam, the foundational motivation is not moral aspiration but obligation management. The system is structured around fear: fear of divine punishment, fear of eternal torment, fear of grave torture, fear of falling short of what is required. The believer is not necessarily invited to grow in virtue but to comply with commands. The message is: *do this or suffer the consequences*. Religious obligations in this framework are not shaped around internal transformation but external accountability. Prayers are not primarily a relational act of communion; they are required actions whose absence carries severe consequences. Charity is not framed as an act of moral empathy, but as a spiritual transaction. Sin is not avoided out of developed moral conscience, but out of fear of hellfire. It is a formulaic system: obey, and you are safe. Disobey, and you are condemned. When any human being is conditioned in this way, when fear is the dominant motivator, certain patterns inevitably emerge. Like the taxi drivers, people learn to aim for the minimum required to avoid negative outcomes. They hit their "target"—five daily prayers, annual fasting, prescribed almsgiving—and then stop. The objective becomes to meet the quota, not to transcend it. Life becomes less about *becoming* and more about *avoiding*.

This has tangible consequences for public life. In Western societies, there is a premium placed on internalized virtue, civic responsibility, and ethical self-determination. Citizens are called to do what is right not out of fear, but out of conscience. The moral framework is aspirational: it calls people to sacrifice, to create, to serve. But when religious and social conditioning are structured around divine surveillance and juridical compliance, the system inevitably trains people to focus on appearances. The question is not "What would serve the common good?" but "What is the minimum necessary?"—and the answer is often found in texts written over a thousand years ago. In such environments, public service becomes transactional. The incentive is not necessarily to lead or inspire, but to fulfill duty, maintain status, or avoid blame.

The economy stagnates because risk-taking is discouraged. Islamic theology teaches that all outcomes—wealth, poverty, success, failure—are decreed by Allah. This deterministic view of life can subtly undermine initiative. If results are preordained, why push further? Policy and lawmaking are similarly impacted. Rather than adjusting to new realities or incorporating empirical evidence, decisions are often constrained by fixed theological boundaries. Laws rooted in divine command are not open to revision. As a result, legal systems in many Muslim-majority contexts struggle to adapt to the moral and technological needs of modernity.

This is not a condemnation of Muslims. It is a structural

analysis. Any person raised within a system where fear is central, over time, internalizes patterns of loss aversion, minimal compliance, and authority dependence. This is a predictable psychological and sociological outcome. A television ad once showed a mother telling her child that the iPad must stay in the playroom and food must stay in the dining room. The child, wanting both, simply sat in the doorway between the two rooms, keeping the food technically in one room and the iPad technically in the other. He followed the rule but circumvented its spirit. This encapsulates a mindset born from legalistic conditioning: if the letter of the law is preserved, then the intent can be ignored.

Islam, with its extensive catalog of do's and don'ts, its focus on jurisprudence over principle, and its promise of reward and punishment based on external compliance, fosters this same approach to morality. It produces individuals trained not to seek what is good, but what is permissible—or more accurately, what is not explicitly forbidden. In such systems, manipulation and deception are not inherently wrong if they remain within the technical bounds of the law. This creates a moral culture obsessed with loopholes, where intentions are irrelevant so long as actions pass the legal test. This not only weakens personal integrity, it undermines entire institutions. And when this mindset is imported into the moral bloodstream of Western civilization, it corrodes the very pillars that sustain it. What began as a religious psychology becomes a societal pathology, quietly dismantling the moral architecture that once made the West flourish.

THE INSTITUTIONALIZATION OF SUBJUGATION

From the earliest years of my life, I was surrounded by a reality that few in the West can truly comprehend. I saw the women in my life beaten not once or twice, but regularly. I saw hair pulled, blood spilled, faces swollen with shame and fists. These weren't rare episodes; they were rhythms of life. My mother, my aunts, my cousins, my neighbors. You might be tempted to say that domestic violence is a global problem, and you would be right. But just as violence is universal and Islam sanctified it, so too is domestic violence universal, but Islam institutionalized it.

In pre-Islamic Arabia, a woman's worth was transactional. She was valued for her womb—an incubator for future soldiers—or for her service to male pleasure. This was the tribal calculus of survival. And contrary to popular Muslim apologetics, Islam did not revolutionize the status of women; it ratified the status quo and fossilized it in scripture. When Muhammad migrated to Medina, the Ansar, his new supporters, divided not only their wealth with the migrants, but their wives. A man with two wives would "generously" give one in marriage to a migrant.[16] The Ansar, for this act, are venerated in the Islamic world to this day. Of course, such acts of objectifying women were not unique to Arabia. But what is unique is their enshrinement into eternity. What was once a desperate custom for survival became sacred altruism in Islam's founding narrative.

Muhammad's own life testified to this view of women. He had over sixty women: fifteen wives and more than forty-five concubines. His companions were limited to four wives, but strategic divorce allowed them to cycle through countless women.[17] His grandson Hasan was famous for divorcing four wives one day and marrying four new ones the next.[18] Muhammad even traded seven concubines for one woman he desired more, Safiyya, handing them to Dihya al-Kalbi in exchange.[19] These weren't just private indulgences. They became aspirational models. The Prophet's life is not interpreted by Muslims as an anomaly—it is the standard. And so, what he did is not only permitted, it is revered.

The theological scaffolding is no less damning. Women are described in the hadith as having half the intellect and half the religion of men. They are ordered to remain in their homes (Qur'an 33:33), to obey without question, to submit entirely. In paradise, women are the reward for men. In war, they are the spoils; conquered cities come with conquered women. In one narration, Muhammad described women as the image of Satan,[20] warning men not to be seduced by them. In another, he declared that if women go to hell, they drag their husbands, brothers, and fathers with them, making women not just moral hazards but collective liabilities. One hadith recounts that Muhammad once saw a woman walking by and was so aroused that he rushed to his wife to relieve himself.[21] The problem wasn't his impulse—it was her existence. That is the ecosystem Islam creates: a world in which male weakness is sanctified, and female presence is criminalized.

When individuals shaped by Islamic patriarchy enter Western systems—as citizens, as parents, as teachers, as policymakers—their internal logic remains. It cannot help but bleed into everything they touch. In schools, girls are pressured to conform to modesty codes not out of self-respect but out of fear of male lust. In homes, boys are taught that their honor rests on their sisters' behavior. In courts, abusers are defended as guardians. In political discourse, critics of these systems are labeled intolerant. The very tools that Western societies use to protect diversity become weapons used against their foundations. A value system that exonerates male aggression, sanctifies female subjugation, and institutionalizes unequal worth cannot peacefully coexist with the Western model. The two are not in dialogue, they are in collision. And the cost of this collision is borne first by the women, then by the culture.

THE CEILING OF MORALITY

Islam's moral ceiling is fixed. It was set in the 7th century, by one man, in one culture, at one moment in history, and it has remained immovable ever since. In Islam, you cannot morally surpass Muhammad. You cannot outgrow him. You cannot call his actions into question. You cannot improve upon his ethics. He is not just the founder of a religion; he is the measuring stick by which all human behavior is judged. And that is the core problem. Muhammad married a child, Aisha, who was nine at consummation, according to the most authoritative Islamic sources. He owned slaves and traded them. He ordered assassinations. He led raids, sanctioned the beheading of prisoners, and permitted the taking of women as war booty. He lied strategically, he permitted polygamy for himself beyond the limit he set for others, and he institutionalized differential rights for men and women. None of it is debated in the tradition. These acts are in the source texts. And because they are his, they are beyond critique.

So, what happens when you build an entire civilization on the unalterable example of a man whose morality reflected the standards of a tribal, pre-modern, warlord society? You freeze ethics in time. You take a snapshot of 7th-century Arabia and make it eternal. You strip future generations of the ability to reach higher. Many Muslims are decent, kind, intelligent human beings. The issue is not individual virtue, it's systemic limitation. Islam's framework does not allow its followers to evolve past its founder. That's the bottleneck. That is why Islamic reform always fails. The ceiling is too low.

What happens when people who sincerely revere such a figure settle in liberal, open societies? They don't simply become pluralistic citizens. Their highest loyalty remains to a system that views secular law as inferior, democracy as optional, free speech as blasphemy, and gender equality as rebellion. The society around them may offer liberties, but their frame tells them these liberties are dangerous. This creates two devastating consequences.

First, the erosion of social cohesion. A society cannot survive if it houses large communities who inwardly reject its principles while outwardly navigating them. Multiculturalism becomes a euphemism for parallel moral universes: one built on evolving ideals of individual rights, and another on immutable divine command tied to a pre-modern context. You cannot build a common life on that contradiction.

Second, the subversion of policy. In democratic societies, population becomes influence. Influence becomes policy. And when officials, activists, or even voters believe that the Prophet's model is ideal, what kind of laws will they advocate for? Speech restrictions. Gender segregation. Halal finance systems. Blasphemy codes disguised as anti-hate legislation. All of it justified not by universal reason, but by fidelity to a man whose ethical playbook is incompatible with the West.

The evidence is not scattered but systemic. A faith that sacralizes violence cannot coexist with a civilization that restrains it. A psychology trained to fear loss and chase reward cannot stand beside one built on conscience and aspiration. A framework that institutionalizes the subjugation of women cannot share space with a culture that enshrines their equality. And a moral ceiling frozen in the 7th century cannot rise to meet a civilization that demands progress. These are not cultural quirks, they are structural incompatibilities. They are not incidental flaws, they are the operating system of Islam. To pretend otherwise is not tolerance, it is denial. And denial in the face of reality is how civilizations lose their future.

CHAPTER 4
REBRANDING ISLAM

THE OVERLAPPING CONSENSUS

Every stable democracy rests on a hidden covenant. It is not a covenant of belief, because no modern society expects its citizens to worship the same God, recite the same creed, or share the same metaphysics, but a covenant of political agreement. It is the shared commitment to certain rules of the game: who makes the laws, how disputes are settled, and which freedoms cannot be revoked. This agreement is the oxygen of the democratic experiment. Remove it, and the whole structure suffocates. The American philosopher John Rawls gave this arrangement a name: the overlapping consensus.[1] He argued that in a modern, pluralistic society, citizens will inevitably hold radically different "comprehensive doctrines"—deep, all-encompassing worldviews, whether religious or secular. The miracle of democracy is that people with utterly divergent moral cosmologies can still live together without civil war if they agree, for their own reasons, on a set of shared political principles. Those principles—equal liberty, equality before the law, freedom of conscience—are, in Rawls's vision, freestanding. They do not hang on the authority of the Bible, the Qur'an, Marx, Nietzsche, or any other singular source. They can be justified from many vantage points and still converge on the same political framework. Even though I have argued before that these so-called "freestanding" liberal democratic principles were, in fact, historically shaped and nurtured by the Judeo-Christian worldview, let us, for the sake of argument, treat them as if they exist independently of any religious or philosophical tradition, available for all to adopt regardless of their cultural or theological roots.

To see how this works, imagine three very different moral tribes:

- **Christians:** They defend equal liberty because every human being is made in the image of God and therefore worthy of protection.
- **Secular humanists:** They defend equal liberty because it safeguards individual autonomy, the right to live by one's own lights without coercion.
- **Utilitarians:** They defend equal liberty because it fosters stability, which maximizes well-being for the greatest number.

They arrive at the same political conclusion for entirely different reasons. That convergence makes peaceful coexistence possible. But Rawls added a non-negotiable qualifier: this overlapping consensus can only hold among *reasonable* doctrines. Reasonableness, in his sense, means you accept the moral fact of pluralism—you acknowledge that other people will reject your worldview, and you agree not to impose your own as binding law unless it is justified in terms that all could, in principle, accept. It is here that the collision with Islam becomes unavoidable. Islam does not merely bring a different comprehensive doctrine to the table; it brings a different *table*. In Islam, sovereignty does not belong to the people. It belongs to Allah alone. The law is not the product of collective deliberation or social contract; it is already given in the Qur'an and embodied in the Sunnah of Muhammad. This law, Sharia, is binding for all people, regardless of whether they believe in it. It is not open to amendment by human will, not even by the unanimous vote of the entire population. From the outset, then, Islam rejects the foundational bargain of liberal democracy.

Muslims in the West claim to "balance" two identities: loyal citizen and faithful Muslim. But this balance is possible only through selective disobedience—either ignoring parts of Islam or ignoring parts of democracy. Follow Islam fully, and you will oppose democratic sovereignty. Follow democracy fully, and you will violate Islam. The two loyalty structures pull in opposite directions. One will eventually override the other. This is why Islam cannot participate in Rawls's overlapping consensus. The bargain requires that when your private creed conflicts with the public framework, you defer to the public framework. But when a doctrine declares, "Our law must govern everyone, and we will change the system when we can," it is no longer part of an overlapping consensus. It is what political theory calls a *modus vivendi*[2]—a truce born of weakness rather than genuine agreement.

The term, Latin for "way of living," entered modern political thought in early modern Europe, when rival states, often with irreconcilable religious or political visions, would agree to a provisional set of rules simply to avoid exhausting themselves in war. These arrangements were pragmatic, not principled; they suspended conflict without resolving it, allowing both sides to survive until one gained the advantage. A *modus vivendi* is therefore not true peace but a pause, a fragile holding pattern that lasts only while both sides find it advantageous, collapsing the moment the balance of power shifts. History demonstrates with unbroken consistency that when Islam gains the strength to enforce its law, it does so without hesitation, because its theological and legal framework demands it. By Rawls's own definition, this makes Islam an unreasonable doctrine: it rejects the democratic bargain at its root, can operate within a democracy when it lacks power, but moves to replace the liberal order entirely when it becomes strong enough. This is not the behavior of a partner in a shared project—it is the behavior of a rival waiting for its opening.

HOW ISLAM RESHAPES DEMOCRATIC SOCIETIES

Rawls's theory tells us Islam cannot truly join a liberal democratic consensus, but political theory alone does not reveal the practical consequences of this incompatibility. How does a small Muslim minority, initially welcomed under the banner of pluralism, become a force that reshapes the host society's political and cultural landscape? The answer lies in a consistent pattern of demographic, cultural, and political transformation, as outlined by Dr. Peter Hammond in his book *Slavery, Terrorism and Islam: The Historical Roots and Contemporary Threat*.[3] Hammond's demographic model, grounded in historical observation and population data, maps the stages through which Muslim communities influence and, over time, transform the societies they enter. This is not to say every Muslim immigrant pursues a political agenda, but rather that Islam, as a totalizing system, operates with remarkable consistency across contexts, leveraging demographic growth and institutional concessions to erode the foundations of liberal democracy.

Hammond's model identifies distinct phases of transformation, tied to the proportion of Muslims in a society's population. Each phase reflects a shift in strategy, from integration to assertion, driven by Islam's theological imperatives and demographic realities.

Phase 1: The Peaceful Minority

When Muslims constitute less than 2% of a population, they present themselves as a peace-loving minority, emphasizing cooperation and integration. This phase is characterized by *da'wah* (missionary work), often framed as cultural exchange or interfaith dialogue. Mosques host open houses, Muslim organizations participate in charity drives, and community leaders emphasize shared values such as compassion or justice. The host society, committed to pluralism, welcomes this outreach—often over-correcting by shielding Islamic doctrine from scrutiny. Laws designed to protect individuals from religious discrimination are repurposed to protect the ideology itself, labeling criticism as bigotry.

Phase 2: Institutional Recognition

As the Muslim population grows to 2–5%, the focus shifts from outreach to securing formal recognition for Islamic practices. Requests for halal food in schools, prayer rooms in workplaces and airports, and recognition of Islamic holidays are framed as civil rights issues. These demands are not mere lifestyle preferences; they signal the assertion of Islamic jurisdiction within public institutions. Each concession sets a precedent, making subsequent refusals politically costly.

Phase 3: Separation and Semi-Autonomy

When the Muslim population reaches 5–10%, a visible shift occurs from integration to separation. Muslim-majority neighborhoods begin to function as semi-autonomous zones, where the host country's laws are only selectively enforced. Informal Sharia courts emerge to handle family disputes, inheritance, and community conflicts, often operating outside the national legal framework. Practices such as forced marriage, honor violence, and female genital mutilation persist, defended as cultural or religious obligations. Law enforcement frequently hesitates to intervene, fearing accusations of discrimination or cultural insensitivity.

When Hammond first outlined his model in 2005, Sweden's Muslim population was about 4–5%, placing it squarely in Phase 2. Two decades later, it has doubled to 8–10%,[4] pushing the country firmly into Phase 3. In Malmö's Rosengård and Stockholm's Rinkeby, Muslim-majority enclaves now operate with their own social rules and community enforcement. Sweden's Police Authority, in its 2021–2024 strategy, identified dozens of "vulnerable areas" where state law is weakened. This is Phase 3 exactly as Hammond described—semi-autonomous zones governed by parallel authority.

Germany has traced the same curve. From 3.7% Muslim in 2005 (about 3 million people) to 6–8% today (5–6 million),[5] it too has crossed into Phase 3. In Berlin's Neukölln and Duisburg's Marxloh, parallel societies have taken shape, where the authority of local "community leaders" rivals that of the state. The 2016 Berlin Christmas market bombing nd the mass mobilizations in 2020 over French cartoons of Muhammad, illustrate Phase 3's defining traits: cultural assertiveness and selective obedience to national law. While Germany has not yet tipped into the sustained violence of Phase 4, the growth of police-designated "no-go zones" and open calls for Sharia-based governance point unmistakably to where the trend is headed.

The UK's trajectory is just as clear. In 2005, 2.7% of the population was Muslim (1.6 million). Today, the figure is between 6.5–7.5% (4.5–5 million),[6] moving from Phase 2 to Phase 3. Tower Hamlets and Bradford now function under semi-autonomous norms that diverge sharply from national law. The 2021 Batley Grammar School incident, where a teacher was driven into hiding after showing a Muhammad cartoon, was a textbook Phase 3 moment: intimidation over blasphemy, speech policed by religious offense, and law enforcement bending to community pressure.

Three countries. Three political systems. Three welfare

regimes. One pattern. Since 2005, all have advanced from accommodation to separation and semi-autonomy in precisely the way Hammond described.

THE MILITIA PHASE

Building on Hammond's framework, I call the next stage the Militia Phase. By the time an Islamic enclave in Western Europe enters Phase 3, semi-autonomy, it already possesses three critical assets:

1 Territorial concentration – dense Muslim-majority neighborhoods where cultural, social, and economic life is organized internally, and outsiders rarely enter.

2 Parallel governance – mosques, community associations, and informal councils functioning as de facto municipal authorities in matters of family, business disputes, and moral conduct.

3 Narrative control – a unified ideological frame that presents Muslims as a collective under siege from systemic Islamophobia, colonial legacies, and cultural oppression.

At this point, day-to-day governance inside the enclave follows Islamic norms more than the host nation's laws. Police enter only in force. Schools push grievance-centered worldviews. Local politicians, often Muslim, serve as intermediaries who extract concessions from the wider government.

The move toward militia formation begins when three conditions align:

• **Heightened grievance.** A triggering event, real or manufactured, provides a rallying cry. This could be a police raid in a criminal investigation, a controversial political statement about Islam, or a violent incident involving far-right extremists. The narrative quickly frames the enclave as the victim of an existential assault.

- **Organizational infrastructure.** The same mosques, youth groups, and charities that handled community organization in Phase 3 now become recruitment and logistics hubs. "Self-defense committees" form, initially unarmed, to patrol streets and "protect" the community from outsiders and law enforcement.
- **External funding and ideological support.** Money and training flow in from abroad, either from Islamic NGOs, Gulf-based patrons, or sympathetic diaspora networks. Some members travel to conflict zones abroad and return with combat experience.

The pretext to bear arms is crucial. In the Western context, outright calls for jihad would trigger swift repression, so the justification must appear defensive and rights-based. The framing mirrors Western civil-rights language: *"We have the right to protect our community from fascist attacks,"* or *"Police brutality against Muslims will not go unanswered."* Small-scale clashes, whether provoked deliberately or not, become "evidence" that the state has abandoned the enclave's safety, legitimizing the creation of armed patrols. Over time, these patrols evolve from unarmed neighborhood watches into fully armed "security units." Firearms may initially be obtained illegally through criminal networks already operating in the area, then later justified as lawful ownership where gun rights exist (e.g., in parts of the U.S.), or smuggled in from abroad in European contexts.

If the state fails to dismantle these armed structures

early, the militia's power grows steadily. What begins as "self-defense" quickly expands into full-spectrum control. Over time, the militia becomes indistinguishable from a governing authority, with its own security forces, courts, and welfare distribution. The enclave transforms into a true state within a state—armed, ideologically cohesive, and self-sustaining. By this stage, the militia no longer merely resists outside authority; it begins to envision itself as an alternative to it. In a matter of decades, the natural trajectory is toward seeking formal recognition, autonomy, or outright independence, citing self-determination and the "right to govern according to our own laws." At that point, dismantling it would require not just a policing operation, but a military confrontation—with all the political costs and international pressure that entails.

To some, the progression from a cultural enclave to an armed militia might sound like dystopian fiction. It isn't. It is the predictable outcome when a growing population holds to a worldview that cannot, by its nature, coexist with the foundations of a liberal democracy. A community whose ultimate loyalty lies with a religious-political system incompatible with secular governance will not remain content under non-Islamic authority forever. In time, it will seek to impose that system, either gradually, through political dominance, or suddenly, through armed control.

Lebanon provides a clear example. Hezbollah emerged in the 1980s claiming to be a "resistance movement" fighting to liberate Palestine and push Israeli forces out of southern Lebanon. That was the sales pitch. In reality, its true aim, rooted in Iran's Islamic Revolution, was to turn

Lebanon into a Shia Islamic state. The Palestinian cause was the perfect rallying cry: emotionally powerful, internationally recognized, and capable of uniting the Lebanese Shia community while winning sympathy from the broader Muslim world. Hezbollah's rise followed a clear sequence. First, it consolidated power in Shia-majority areas. Next, it built parallel institutions—schools, charities, clinics, and religious courts—that often functioned more effectively than the Lebanese state. Then, under the banner of "resistance," it armed itself, eventually reaching military parity with the national army in its strongholds. By that point, Hezbollah was no longer just a militia, it was the governing authority in its territories, a state within a state.

THE VULNERABILITY OF THE WEST

Any serious attempt by a non-Muslim government to confront armed Islamic factions will be framed, not only domestically but across the world, as persecution of Muslims. This is not theory; it is a proven political weapon, deployed repeatedly to delegitimize a state's right to defend its sovereignty.

In the 1970s in Jordan, Palestinian militias transformed refugee camps into armed strongholds. These factions were operating as a state within a state: collecting taxes, enforcing their own laws, and openly challenging the authority of King Hussein's government. Skirmishes with the Jordanian army escalated into full-scale urban warfare during what became known as Black September. Hussein's Sunni Muslim army moved with overwhelming force, expelling the PLO leadership and dismantling its armed presence. Thousands of Palestinians were killed or expelled—yet the wider Muslim world's reaction was muted. Why? Because it was Muslims fighting Muslims. There was no religious-persecution narrative to weaponize, no *"Christian versus Muslim"* framing to ignite outrage across the Islamic world.

Now compare that to Lebanon just a few years later. Heavily armed Palestinian factions, many of the same groups expelled from Jordan, relocated to southern Lebanon and Beirut's refugee camps. They established parallel governance structures: their own courts, police forces, taxation systems, and military training camps. Their justification was identical to what they had claimed in Jordan—*resistance* against Israel—but in practice they were undermining Lebanese sovereignty and destabilizing the state. When Lebanon's Christian-led government finally moved to confront them in 1975–1976, the reaction was radically different from the Jordan case. Because this time it was a Christian-dominated army facing off against armed Muslim factions, the conflict was instantly reframed as *"Christians massacring Muslims."* Condemnations poured in from across the Islamic world. Arab League summits denounced Lebanon's government. Media in Muslim-majority countries depicted the battle not as an internal security operation, but as religious oppression. This external political pressure constrained Lebanon's military options and deepened the country's fragmentation, laying the groundwork for the protracted Lebanese Civil War.

The lesson here is brutally simple: when a Muslim-majority government confronts an armed Islamic force, the reaction in the Muslim world is muted; when a non-

Muslim-led government does the same, the reaction is explosive.

Israel has been on the receiving end of this dynamic since its founding in 1948. Every conflict, no matter how clearly defensive in nature, is portrayed as an aggressive, colonial assault on Muslims. Whether in the 1948 War of Independence, the Six-Day War, or operations against Hamas and Hezbollah, the pattern is identical: the initial aggression of armed Islamic factions is erased from the narrative, and the state's defensive response is cast as systemic persecution. The same machinery that has kept Israel under permanent accusation for defending itself can be, and will be, deployed against any Western nation that finds itself confronting an entrenched, armed Muslim enclave on its own soil. The facts will be irrelevant. The narrative will be set before the first shot is fired: the state is the oppressor, the enclave is the victim, and any use of force will be framed as persecution. Once that framing takes hold, the state will find itself fighting not only a militia at home, but a coordinated international political campaign abroad.

Western democracies are particularly ill-equipped to handle this kind of confrontation. The combination of liberal legal systems, free press, and electoral politics creates an environment where perception often matters more than reality. Governments must operate under intense domestic scrutiny, with opposition parties, activist organizations, and media outlets ready to amplify any claim of discrimination or state overreach. In the age of social media, a single incident—whether genuine or staged—can be broadcast globally within minutes, complete with selective footage and emotional narratives that mobilize both local protestors and international diplomatic pressure. Unlike Jordan in 1970 or even Lebanon in the 1970s, Western states have self-imposed legal and moral restraints that Islamic factions can weaponize. Hate-speech laws, anti-discrimination statutes, and broad protections for religious expression make it politically costly to target Islamic networks, even when those networks are openly subverting the state. Law enforcement agencies already tread lightly in Muslim-majority neighborhoods for fear of triggering unrest or being accused of profiling. Once an enclave develops the capacity to arm itself under a "self-defense" narrative, the political and legal culture of the West makes decisive early intervention far less likely. This delay is exactly what allows a militia to consolidate power —until the cost of removing it is no longer merely political, but measured in blood.

WHY THE WEST WON'T TAKE ISLAM AT ITS WORD

There are thousands of videos of Muslim clerics in Western countries saying openly what this chapter has outlined: calls for Sharia supremacy, rejection of secular law, and the eventual dominance of Islam over every other system. These messages are delivered in mosques, shouted in demonstrations, posted online, and repeated in community meetings. They come not only from fringe figures, but from established community leaders, registered organizations, and ordinary imams operating openly under Western laws.

Despite this, Western governments and media respond with disbelief or dismissal. The problem is not that Islam hides its political objectives—it does not. The problem is that the West refuses to accept them at face value. This blindness stems from deeply rooted habits in Western thinking: projecting its own values onto others, carrying the burden of post-colonial guilt, succumbing to ideological blindness, and suffering from a profound loss of cultural self-confidence.

The shadow of Nazism and fascism left the West deeply wary of labeling any ideology as inherently dangerous. Combined with guilt over colonialism and slavery, the moral reflex now is to assume the West—not Islam—is the aggressor. Many policymakers see Islamic supremacism not as an ideological threat, but as a symptom of "grievances" to be solved with aid, integration, and messaging.

Post-colonial theory adds another layer of protection for Islam. In Western academia and politics, criticism of non-Western cultures, especially Islam, is cast as racism or colonial arrogance. The label *Islamophobe* can discredit individuals and movements instantly, making confrontation politically costly. Accommodation becomes the path of least resistance—which, in Islamic political logic, is simply the first step toward submission.

The West also misreads Islamic solidarity. Whereas Western societies moved from tribal loyalty to civic nationalism, Islam remains tied to the *ummah*, a global political community bound by divine law. Loyalty is not to a flag or constitution but to Allah's commands. The West assumes Islam functions like Christianity after its separation of church and state. This leads to a fatal misunderstanding of power: Westerners believe kindness builds trust, but in Islamic political culture, respect flows from strength. Concessions signal weakness, encouraging further demands—always a step toward more influence, never an endpoint.

The deeper problem is the West's crisis of conviction. Islam still believes in its mission. The West, steeped in moral relativism, no longer believes in the superiority of its own political order. It doubts whether it even should defend itself. And without the will, the means are irrelevant. Comfort has replaced sacrifice as the West's civic virtue. Islam demands struggle; the West avoids inconvenience. One side is willing to die for its vision; the other is reluctant to risk social disapproval. In such an asymmetry, the outcome is not hard to predict.

But the main reason the West does not believe Muslims when they declare their supremacist ambitions is that Islam itself has been absolved of responsibility for them. This absolution came through the manufactured framing of Islamic jihad and supremacy as a separate political movement that supposedly emerged in the mid-20th century. By labeling it *Islamism*, Western academics, journalists, and policymakers recast the drive for Sharia rule and global Islamic dominance as a modern political phenomenon, detached from the religion's core teachings and history.

This framing has been the perfect shield. Terrorism, militancy, and parallel governance could be condemned without ever confronting the theological source that has fueled them for over a millennium. Therefore, if Islam is truly a religion of peace and "Islamism" is the real problem, the conclusion follows that the rhetoric of Islamists should not alarm us. They would be, by definition, a fringe minority—loud, perhaps dangerous in isolated cases, but unrepresentative of the overwhelming majority of Muslims who supposedly want to live quietly and coexist peacefully within Western societies.

That is exactly the reassurance this framing delivers to policymakers, media, and the public. It turns the most explicit calls for Sharia supremacy, jihad, and dismantling of secular law into something akin to neo-Nazi leaflets or anarchist manifestos: distasteful but not existential. As a result, the West treats these declarations not as warnings, but as noise. Islam speaks with clarity—but the West has trained itself not to listen.

ISLAM VS. ISLAMISM

In the 19th century, European orientalists used the term *Islamism* to describe the study of Islam or the religion itself, much like *Buddhism* or *Hinduism*.[7] It was a neutral academic label, not a political one. By the early 20th century, Western scholars and administrators started using *Islamism* to describe what they saw as a politicized form of Islam—essentially, as we discussed earlier, groups seeking to reestablish the Caliphate.

This was the first step in a deliberate redefinition: casting Islam's political ambitions as a modern, aberrant strain rather than an intrinsic feature. By the mid-20th century, with the rise of figures like Sayyid Qutb and the Muslim Brotherhood, *Islamism* was fully recast as a distinct ideology, a supposed perversion of Islam that sought to impose Sharia and establish Islamic governance. This redefinition peaked after 9/11, when the West's fear of being labeled Islamophobic reached fever pitch. Media and politicians leaned hard into the Islam-versus-Islamism narrative, insisting that *Islamism* was a political ideology divorced from the "spiritual" essence of Islam.

For nearly two decades, I lived as a Muslim. I never even heard the term *Islamism* until I began interacting with Western academics and media. To a Muslim living by the Qur'an and Sunnah, it is meaningless. No serious Islamic scholar teaches that there is a separate category of Muslim called an *Islamist*. There is only the Muslim who obeys Allah and His Messenger, and the Muslim who fails to do so.

In other words, the so-called *Islamist* is simply the Muslim who takes the religion seriously—who doesn't pick and choose, who applies Islam to every part of life. A nominal Christian can reject biblical commands on sexuality, the exclusivity of Christ, or the authority of Scripture and still be recognized by other Christians as part of the faith. A Jew can reject the divine origin of the Torah, or the authority of the Talmud, and still be embraced in Jewish community. There is theological space for pluralism.

Islam allows no such luxury. The Qur'an is the literal, eternal word of Allah. Muhammad is the perfect example for all mankind until the end of time. The Hadiths are binding. To reject them is to leave Islam. Even Qur'anists, the tiny minority who accept only the Qur'an and reject the Hadiths, are considered apostates by the rest of the Muslim world. This unity on the fundamentals is why the "moderate Muslim" vs. "Islamist" binary is so misleading.

The various sects—Sunni, Shia, Ibadi—may differ on who should have succeeded Muhammad or how certain rituals are performed, but they do not differ on the necessity of Sharia, the authority of the Qur'an, the obligation of jihad, or the supremacy of Islam over all other systems. Those are the points that define *Islamism* in Western parlance, and they are also the points that define Islam itself.

The West, however, needed the term. The atrocities of al-Qaeda and ISIS were so graphic, so impossible to sanitize, that Western apologists for Islam had to come up with a way to condemn the acts without condemning the theology that inspired them. Thus, *Islamism* became the escape hatch—a way to say, *"This isn't Islam, it's a radical political movement."* And once that framing took hold, Islam itself was absolved.

But by pretending that *Islamism* is the problem, the West blinds itself to the real source of the threat. It ends up banning groups while leaving the ideology that produces them untouched. It condemns the bombings while protecting the scripture that commands them. It fights the symptoms while shielding the disease. And in doing so, it does Muslims no favors. You cannot reform what you refuse to diagnose. If you keep telling Muslims that Islam is peaceful and that only *Islamism* is the problem, they will never feel the need to examine the doctrines that make *Islamism* inevitable.

Islam, as we have seen, is political by nature. It always has been. If an *Islamist* is defined as someone who seeks to implement Islam as a political system, then Muhammad himself was the first Islamist, and every devout Muslim is commanded to follow his example. The distinction between Islam and Islamism collapses under even the most basic doctrinal test. *Islamism* is simply Islam with no brakes. It is Islam applied.

You only need to accept the Qur'an and Sunnah as the ultimate standard for all human life to become what is called an Islamist. The first Islamist was Muhammad. Every Muslim who seeks to follow him fully—whether by preaching, lobbying, building parallel societies, or waging armed jihad—is walking the same path. The only difference between the "Islamist" and the "Muslim" is the degree to which they have the freedom, power, and will to act on what they believe.

That's why the West's linguistic firewall between Islam and Islamism is not only false but dangerous. It gives cover to those who share the ideology but have not yet, or cannot yet, translate it into force. By insisting that Islam is innocent and only *Islamism* is the problem, the West has built a wall of moral immunity around the doctrine itself. This absolves Muslims of confronting the supremacist elements in their faith, because the West has already declared those elements to be alien to Islam.

The result is a closed loop: every jihadist act is reframed as *"not true Islam"*—and therefore Islam requires no reform.

You might ask: *What's the problem, then?* Even if this modern, sanitized version of Islam isn't fully rooted in theology, hasn't it at least established itself as a peaceful, practical alternative? Isn't that a step forward?

The answer is no. Not even close. In fact, it's worse than useless; it's dangerous. When a Muslim embraces this rebranded Islam while insisting that it is the true Islam, he becomes an unwitting shield for the very sources—the Qur'an, the Hadith, and the classical jurisprudence—that Islamic terrorists openly cite as their mandate. He doesn't dismantle the machinery that produces jihad; he defends it.

By declaring, *"This is Islam, and it is peaceful,"* he grants those same sacred texts an unearned immunity from criticism. In doing so, he fortifies the soil from which every so-called *Islamist* movement grows.

If Muslims openly admitted that their modernized version requires modifying, reinterpreting, or discarding major parts of the original tradition, that would be progress. It would at least create an honest distinction between the historical faith and the moral reforms necessary to live in a pluralistic society. But that's not what's happening.

That's why the world still struggles to identify—let alone confront—the real power source behind global jihad. The followers of this fabricated Islam refuse to allow serious questions about the texts themselves, because such questions would expose that their *"peaceful Islam"* is only possible by rejecting core tenets of the faith. As long as the mask is mistaken for the face, the ideology that fuels the violence remains sacred, untouchable, and ready to be activated by anyone willing to remove the mask.

In this way, the so-called *moderates* become the unintentional bodyguards of the very system they claim to oppose.

THE CASE AGAINST ISLAMOPHOBIA

In the modern Western lexicon, *"Islamophobia"* has become a weapon—designed, refined, and deployed to neutralize criticism of Islam before it can even begin. The term doesn't simply mean *"hatred of Muslims"* as its defenders claim. In practice, it means that Islam as an ideology is placed off-limits for scrutiny. That is its true function.

The core manipulation of *Islamophobia* is that it treats the fear of an ideology as morally equivalent to irrational prejudice against people. But fearing a political-religious system that openly declares its supremacy over all others is not irrational—it is prudent. Fear becomes irrational only when it is baseless, and the case against Islamic supremacism is anything but baseless. Islam's political theology is not hidden. It has been consistent for over 1,400 years: Islam is the final, perfect system, meant for every place and every time, destined to rule all others. To fear the legal and political consequences of that worldview is no different than fearing totalitarianism, fascism, or communism. Yet by branding such fear as a *phobia,* the term smuggles in the idea that it is irrational, baseless, and morally disreputable. That's the power of the word: it forces a moral concession before the conversation even starts.

The West has been conditioned to see bigotry and criticism as synonymous. Once that conflation took hold, all that was required to make Islam immune to critique was to present it as a racial or cultural identity rather than a belief system. The moment you racialize a religion, you can frame every challenge to its doctrines as a form of racial discrimination. It is a brilliant maneuver, and it has worked almost flawlessly.

But Islam has no race. It includes Black Nigerians, white Bosnians, Malay Indonesians, Arab Yemenis, and blue-eyed London converts. Yet in Western political discourse, Islam is packaged into a single visual stereotype: brown-skinned, immigrant, hijab-wearing. This is deliberate. The moment a religion is recast as an ethnic identity, it becomes shielded by the moral firewall that protects minorities from racial prejudice. Once that shield is in place, everything changes. Objecting to Sharia law is no longer a defense of liberal democracy—it's "punching down" on an oppressed minority. Condemning honor killings or child marriage is reframed as cultural intolerance. Even challenging the idea of parallel legal systems is portrayed as an attack on *"inclusion"* and *"diversity."*

The power of this framing is that it inverts the moral high ground. The critic becomes the villain, and the ideology becomes the victim.

In the late 20th century, cultural relativism told the West that no culture could be judged by another's standards. The net effect was paralysis—the inability to defend universal human rights without being accused of cultural arrogance. *Islamophobia* is simply the updated, more aggressive version of that paralysis. Where cultural relativism said, *"You can't judge their culture,"* Islamophobia says, *"You're a bigot if you do."* And it comes with teeth: social ostracism, loss of employment, legal consequences in some jurisdictions, and public humiliation. The goal is to make the cost of speaking out so high that most people will choose silence.

Consider the double standard: if any other religious or political text today called for the execution of apostates, the enslavement of captives, or the subjugation of all non-believers, it would be banned as extremist hate literature. If any other religion taught that Jews and Christians should be fought until they submit, it would be denounced globally as incitement. The Qur'an and Hadith contain exactly these prescriptions, and yet they are not only protected but revered. Why? Because calling them out triggers the *Islamophobia* alarm. The conversation ends before it begins, and the ideology remains untouchable.

Islamophobia is not about protecting Muslims from hate crimes; laws against violence already exist for that. It is about making you doubt your right to criticize an ideology. It is about training you to see legitimate scrutiny as moral failing, so that you self-censor before you ever speak.

The genius of this tactic is that it doesn't have to outlaw criticism—it makes you police yourself. It doesn't have to criminalize dissent—it makes dissent socially fatal. It weaponizes your own values—tolerance, pluralism, anti-racism—against you.

This is why *Islamophobia* is the perfect shield. It doesn't just defend Islam from bigotry; it defends it from scrutiny. And without scrutiny, the ideology's political ambitions can advance unopposed, under the cover of victimhood.

THE REBRANDING OF ISLAMIC JIHAD

Manufacturing *Islamism* to shield Islam from the catastrophic ramifications of jihad worldwide, coupled with the weaponization of *Islamophobia,* created a climate where Islam could advance within Western institutions under the cover of victimhood. Yet Western naïveté—the gift that keeps on giving—granted Islam an additional layer of absolution by rebranding jihad itself. The very mechanism of Islam's expansion was given a makeover for Western audiences. What had been an unapologetic doctrine of armed supremacy for over a millennium, was repackaged through a mix of geopolitical maneuvering, ideological agendas, and cultural concessions.

During the Cold War, Western powers, led by the United States, weaponized jihadist movements to counter Soviet expansion. In the 1980s, the Afghan mujahideen—armed and funded by the CIA to resist Soviet occupation—were celebrated as heroic *freedom fighters*. This required recasting jihad as a noble struggle against tyranny, stripped of its theological roots in violence and supremacy. Operation Cyclone, which funneled billions to Islamic groups, relied on euphemisms to reassure Western audiences uneasy about aiding religious extremists. After the Cold War, the West continued to utilize jihadist factions in later conflicts, including the Bosnian War (1992–1995) and the Syrian Civil War (2011–2024), where groups like Jabhat al-Nusra benefited from indirect Western support. The same sanitized framing of jihad remained in play because it served Western geopolitical interests.

However, this cooperation was later distorted into the claim that Western foreign policy had *created* Islamic jihad itself. That conflation became a potent propaganda tool, pushed by Islamic apologists and amplified by the political left, shifting blame away from Islamic ideology and onto the West. While Western policy certainly exploited jihadist groups for strategic ends, that is not the same as manufacturing them from nothing. The West has made catastrophic mistakes—such as the Trump administration's May 2025 decision to grant legitimacy to the new ISIS government in Syria—but in every case, it was tapping into what Islam had already produced, not inventing something new.

Meanwhile, Western academia was being reshaped by the intellectual currents of multiculturalism and post-colonialism, movements that gained momentum in the 1960s and 1970s and later converged with Cold War–era rebranding efforts. Rather than acknowledging jihad's codified role in Islamic jurisprudence as an obligation of armed struggle to expand Islamic rule, scholars selectively highlighted fringe or minority interpretations, portraying jihad as a personal moral effort, a campaign for social justice, or a form of anti-colonial resistance. These reframings leaned on decontextualized Quranic verses or marginal Sufi traditions, while downplaying the overwhelmingly martial treatment of jihad in the Qur'an, Hadith, and classical legal manuals.

The motive was political and social: to promote integration of growing Muslim immigrant populations in Europe and North America, to defuse cultural tensions, and to insulate Muslim communities from suspicion or hostility. By casting jihad in benign, even noble terms, this academic trend aligned neatly with broader narratives of inclusivity and cultural relativism. Over time, universities and policy-oriented think tanks became echo chambers for these sanitized interpretations, cultivating a generation of journalists, diplomats, and policymakers who internalized the rebranded view of jihad. The cumulative effect was the normalization of the idea that jihad could be compatible with liberal democratic values—an idea sustained only by suppressing serious engagement with the doctrinal imperatives and historical record of conquest, subjugation, and religious supremacy that had defined it for over a millennium.

The September 11, 2001 attacks, carried out by al-Qaeda explicitly in the name of jihad, thrust the term into Western consciousness with unprecedented force, cementing its link to catastrophic violence. In the aftermath, Western leaders, fearing domestic unrest and the alienation of Muslim populations, leaned heavily on academics and policy advisors to sever jihad from terrorism. President George W. Bush's declaration that *"Islam is a religion of peace"* became the flagship talking point, framing jihadists not as faithful executors of a well-documented doctrine but as aberrations who had "hijacked" a noble faith.

This fear-driven revisionism was swiftly institutionalized. In both the United States and the United Kingdom, official reports and policy papers began systematically referring to jihadists as *Islamists,* a semantic shift that blurred the doctrinal specificity of jihad and recast it as a fringe political ideology rather than a mainstream religious obligation. Counterterrorism strategies—such as those utilized in the UK's Prevent program and the U.S. Department of Homeland Security's post-9/11 plan—consciously avoided terminology that might link violence to Islamic theology.[8] Instead, they adopted the sanitized language of *"violent extremism"* as a generic phenomenon, deliberately detaching it from its scriptural and historical roots.

THE MECHANISM OF REBRANDING

The transformation of jihad's meaning in the Western mind was the product of a deliberate convergence between Muslims living in the West and certain Western ideological currents. Muslims navigating life in pluralistic societies needed a way to shield their faith from direct association with violence without disavowing its theological roots. For segments of Western academia and political culture, Islam became a convenient ally—a living counter-narrative to Western dominance—whose historical grievances and claims to victimhood fit neatly within prevailing critiques of power, empire, and "Eurocentric" narratives. This mutual accommodation created a climate in which the historical and textual realities of jihad could be quietly set aside in favor of interpretations that advanced both identity politics and geopolitical agendas.

One of the most persistent revisionist claims reframes jihad as an imperialist distortion of Islam, a narrative rooted in Edward Said's *Orientalism* (1978) and reinforced by scholars such as Rashid Khalidi and others.[9] This framework asserts that Western portrayals of jihad as violent are merely colonial constructs, fabricated to paint Islam as inherently belligerent and to justify imperial domination. According to this view, Orientalist scholars intentionally exaggerated jihad's militancy to dehumanize Muslims and rationalize European conquests, from British rule in India to French occupation in Algeria. The driving force behind this claim is post-colonial guilt and entrenched anti-Western sentiment. Said, Khalidi, and others working within a Marxist-influenced critique of power sought to invert the historical narrative: the West becomes the eternal aggressor, and Islam the perpetual victim. By framing jihad's long record of conquest as a colonial myth, they aimed simultaneously to rehabilitate Islam's image and to indict Western imperialism.

Another revisionist narrative, pushed heavily by Muslim apologists and embraced in the West by figures like Karen Armstrong, John L. Esposito, and other sympathetic scholars, portrays jihad as nothing more than defensive warfare,[10] waged only when Muslims faced imminent danger. In this telling, Muhammad's campaigns—from Badr and Uhud to the Trench—are framed as reluctant measures to protect a besieged community rather than calculated steps in a larger expansionist project. Later Islamic conquests are rebranded as preemptive security operations or humanitarian liberations, never as imperial ventures. This version has been smuggled into school textbooks, government counter-extremism programs, interfaith initiatives, and media guidelines, ensuring that "jihad" is heard through the moral filter of self-defense rather than its original legal and theological framework.

A third revisionist narrative claims that jihad's primary and most important meaning is an inner spiritual struggle against personal weaknesses rather than armed conflict. Figures such as John Esposito and Annemarie Schimmel popularized this reframing, presenting jihad as a moral exercise akin to Christian asceticism or Buddhist meditation. In this telling, jihad becomes an inspirational, private discipline with universal appeal—something that could belong in a self-help seminar rather than on a battlefield. But this entire reinterpretation rests on a single hadith, often paraphrased as, *"We have returned from the lesser jihad to the greater jihad, the struggle against the self."*[11] This hadith does not appear in any of Islam's six canonical collections (*Sahih al-Bukhari, Sahih Muslim, Sunan Abu Dawud, Jami' al-Tirmidhi, Sunan al-Nasa'i,* or *Sunan Ibn Majah*). Classical authorities such as Ibn Hajar al-Asqalani have deemed it weak (*da'if*), while others have classified it as outright fabricated. It is, in other words, a fringe anecdote elevated far beyond its original stature to redefine one of Islam's most central doctrines. By contrast, in the Qur'an jihad is framed almost exclusively as armed conquest, a divinely mandated struggle to expand Islamic rule, and in the two most authoritative Hadith collections, *Sahih al-Bukhari* and *Sahih Muslim,* the term "jihad" appears nearly 200 times—and every reference concerns armed struggle.

A particularly resilient strain of revisionism, championed by figures such as Tariq Ramadan, Saba Mahmood, and Talal Asad, has reimagined jihad through three overlapping lenses: as a struggle for social justice, as resistance to Western imperialism, and as a reaction to socio-political grievances. This composite narrative strips jihad of its supremacist theological core and dresses it in the language of modern political activism. In these narratives, jihad becomes a moral crusade against inequality, akin to the U.S. civil rights movement or anti-apartheid campaigns. Jihadist violence is recast as the inevitable backlash of colonized peoples against Western domination. And jihad loses its doctrinal grounding altogether, reduced to a desperate response to poverty, marginalization, or foreign intervention.

This reframing operates as an ideological triple shield.

The social justice angle plugs Islam into the moral prestige of progressive activism, making jihad relatable to Western audiences already invested in anti-racist and anti-capitalist struggles. The anti-imperial lens flips the moral polarity, transforming the jihadist from aggressor to victim and the West from defender to oppressor. The socio-political grievance frame then seals the argument by suggesting that jihadist violence would disappear if only economic disparities, political exclusions, or Western interventions were addressed. Taken together, these approaches launder jihad's image entirely—presenting it not as the explicit, text-driven religious obligation it always was, but as a noble, if sometimes misapplied, reaction to injustice.

WHY IS IT DANGEROUS?

By obscuring jihad's theological roots, revisionism emboldens groups like ISIS, al-Qaeda, and Boko Haram, who explicitly draw their legitimacy from the Qur'an and Muhammad's campaigns. The failure to confront this link —seen in Western reluctance to label attacks like the 2015 *Charlie Hebdo* massacre as jihadist—grants extremists the very cover they need. It allows them to present themselves not as aberrations but as faithful executors of divine command, radicalizing vulnerable populations under the banner of theological authenticity.

Denying jihad's religious basis cripples counterterrorism. Policies that focus narrowly on socio-economic grievances, as seen in Britain's post-2005 London bombings response, consistently miss the core driver: the doctrinal mandate of jihad. Attacks like the 2020 Vienna shooting were not born from poverty or alienation but from scriptural imperatives. By misdiagnosing the cause, Western societies leave themselves vulnerable to a violence that thrives not on deprivation but on revelation.

The fear of being accused of Islamophobia further stifles honest discourse, weakening Western resolve to confront jihadist ideologies directly. This dynamic has been evident in Europe's muted response to repeated terrorist attacks, where media outlets and political leaders avoid linking jihad to Islam. Such self-censorship does not preserve pluralism; it corrodes it. It signals to jihadists that the West is unwilling to name the ideology that fuels their war, undermining the very defense of liberal values against theocratic threats.

Sanitized narratives also erase the memory of jihad's victims: the Buddhists of Afghanistan, the Jews of Arabia, the Sikhs of Punjab, and countless others whose civilizations were decimated in Islam's expansion. This amnesia dishonors their legacy and distorts the historical record. It leaves modern societies ignorant of the very forces that shaped the world they inhabit, blinding them to the reality that jihad is not a relic of the past but a persistent, theological engine still driving conflict today.

THE UNHOLY ALLIANCE

The ideological reframing of jihad was never just an academic parlor game or a media trend; it became the bridge that joined Islam to the radical left. Once jihad could be marketed to Western audiences as a struggle for justice, liberation, and resistance—rather than a theological mandate for conquest—it slipped seamlessly into the activist vocabulary of the modern left. From that moment, the alliance was all but inevitable. This was not a union of values but a union of utility. Both sides knew that, left to operate in isolation, their visions of the future would ultimately clash. But in the short term, they recognized a shared enemy: the cultural, political, and moral foundations of Western civilization.

The result was an *unholy alliance*[12] between the West's most illiberal religious ideology and its most self-destructive political movement. For the left, Islam was a strategic windfall. The left's power depends on cultivating and amplifying narratives of victimhood, and Islam came with a ready-made archive of grievance—colonial encounters, wars, Orientalist scholarship—that fit neatly into the intersectional hierarchy of "the oppressed." Especially in the post-9/11 era, Muslims became the perfect political foot soldiers in the left's perpetual campaign against the West, mobilized under banners of anti-racism, anti-imperialism, and "equity." The left's hostility toward Christianity, viewed as the cultural backbone of the West, made Islam even more attractive as a partner. For centuries, Islam positioned itself as Christianity's rival and opponent; in the left's hands, that rivalry could be weaponized to erode Christian moral authority in the public sphere.

But demographics were just as important as ideology. The left knows that the native Western electorate is unlikely to fully embrace radical progressivism. Large-scale immigration from Islamic countries shifts the voting landscape, importing constituencies more receptive to big government, collectivist economics, and identity-driven politics. And the left's instinct for censorship found a natural counterpart in Islam's prohibition against blasphemy. By redefining any criticism of Islam as "Islamophobia" or racist hate speech, they created a ready-made mechanism for speech control, enforceable both legally and socially.

Islam, however, is no passive passenger in this arrangement. It is an active, calculating partner that uses the left's platforms, laws, and cultural influence to advance its own objectives. Leftist demands for "hate speech laws," "cultural sensitivity," and "diversity compliance" function as Trojan horses for Islamic blasphemy codes. Once criticism of Islam is criminalized or driven underground, one of the West's core pillars—free expression—is breached. Through this alliance, Muslims in the West have secured influence in policymaking bodies, academia, media, and even law enforcement. Framed as "community representatives" and "diversity advocates," they gain leverage over how Islam is discussed, portrayed, and legislated. Meanwhile, the left's open-borders agenda accelerates the creation of Muslim-majority enclaves in Western cities, areas where Islamic norms, not Western laws, increasingly dictate social life.

At the same time, Muslims have mastered the art of adopting progressive language for strategic camouflage. They attach themselves to feminist, LGBTQ, or anti-racist causes to rebrand Islam as compatible with progressive values. In doing so, they secure the left's protection while advancing a theocratic project that fundamentally contradicts those movements' stated goals.

History shows where this ends. Islam has never

remained in partnership with non-Islamic forces once it gains the upper hand. The 1979 Iranian Revolution is the clearest modern example: leftist and Islamic factions united to overthrow the Shah, but once the Muslims seized control, they purged, imprisoned, and executed their leftist allies. The same fate awaits today's radical feminists, LGBTQ activists, and socialist revolutionaries who imagine they are paving the road to equality. They will find themselves silenced—or worse—once Islamic objectives are secured.

WHY ISLAM HARDENS IN THE WEST

Muslims who were casual, secular, or even indifferent to their faith back home often become visibly devout, politically active, and more ideologically rigid after settling in the West. Young men who never prayed in their countries of origin suddenly perform all five prayers at work or on campus. Women who never wore the hijab in Damascus veil in Detroit. Mosques that were sparsely attended in their homelands are packed on Fridays in Paris, Toronto, and Sydney. This shift is the result of how identity functions in a minority context—and how well-funded Islamic organizations, backed by foreign governments, have learned to weaponize that identity.

In much of the Muslim world, Islam functions as the default operating system. Religious observance often devolves into an empty checklist—pray, fast, wash, repeat —performed out of social pressure rather than conviction. The constant threat of failure before Allah, coupled with the absence of grace or forgiveness, produces guilt and fatigue. People go through the motions because everyone else does. But when a Muslim moves into the heart of a non-Muslim society, the entire dynamic changes. Suddenly, those same rituals become declarations of loyalty. Praying at the mall or in a public park is no longer just duty—it is a signal: *I am Muslim, even here.* Wearing the hijab becomes not just tradition but a flag. Going to the mosque, organizing events, or proselytizing is recast as active service to Allah behind enemy lines. In the West, Islamic practice acquires new purpose: you are no longer one of millions in a Muslim-majority context; you are now a soldier of the *ummah*, proving your allegiance in the land of the *kuffar*.

Sociologists call this "boundary maintenance." When a minority community fears assimilation, it raises the fences. Leaders, parents, and local clerics demand stricter adherence to religious rules than people might face back home. The paradox is striking: the West doesn't soften Islam—it hardens it. A Muslim who might have lived loosely under Islam in his homeland can find himself pulled toward a stricter, more politicized version once abroad, because now religion is his anchor of identity in a sea of difference.

This hardening process would be limited without infrastructure—but the infrastructure is there. Between 1982 and 2005, Saudi Arabia alone spent more than $75 billion spreading Salafi-Wahhabi Islam worldwide, including the construction of 1,500 mosques, 210 Islamic centers, 200 Islamic colleges, and 2,000 schools in non-Muslim countries. Much of this infrastructure went directly into Western cities. A European Parliament estimate put Saudi spending on Salafi missionary activities at

$10 billion through organizations like the Muslim World League, with Europe as a primary target.[13]

Between 2004 and 2019, Qatar channeled €770 million into 288 organizations across Europe and North America — mosques, Islamic centers, and charities. Over €2 million went to the Örebro Mosque in Sweden, a site tied to ISIS recruitment. Another project was the al-Muhsinin Mosque in Bonn, Germany, associated with al-Qaeda sympathizers. In parallel, Qatar poured over $1 billion into Georgetown University since 2005 to shape Islamic studies at the academic level, while also funding hundreds of projects across Texas universities.[14]

Turkey's Diyanet, backed by a $3.5 billion budget in 2025, has built dozens of mega-mosques abroad, including the $110 million Diyanet Center of America just outside Washington, D.C.[15]

Iran, for its part, uses its Shia networks in Europe and the U.S. through mosques and cultural centers like the Hamburg Islamic Center, funneling resources that tie Western Shia communities directly back to Tehran.[16]

The institutions built by these states function as ideological fortresses, shielding young Muslims from Western influence and binding them to a transnational Islamic identity. Their imams are often trained abroad in hardline seminaries. Their curricula lean heavily on jurisprudence that treats Sharia as a living, mandatory system meant to replace secular law. The messaging is consistent: *the West is morally bankrupt, Muslims are under siege, and your role here is to defend and expand Islam.*

Liberal democracies unintentionally give these organizations exactly what they need: legal protections, funding loopholes, and a climate of fear around criticism. In this environment, what begins as an immigrant religious community can rapidly become a politically mobilized bloc. Protests over foreign conflicts are organized locally. School boards are pressured to revise curricula. Media is flooded with complaints about "offensive" content. Politicians learn quickly that criticizing Islamic doctrines, even indirectly, carries career-ending risks. The long-term result is a self-reinforcing cycle: stricter identity → stronger institutions → more political influence → greater leverage to enforce stricter identity. Each generation grows up further removed from assimilation and more connected to a global Islamic narrative that transcends national loyalty.

Two decades ago, many Muslim families in the West moved back to their countries of origin when their children reached their teenage years, fearing the corrupting influence of Western liberalism. That practice has sharply declined—not because parents stopped worrying, but because Islamic institutions in the West are now robust enough to raise devout, ideologically committed children without sending them "home." The West itself can now be turned into a safe incubator for Islamic identity, provided the infrastructure remains in place.

CHAPTER 5
THE FOREIGN GOD

DEFEATED GODS

Right before the Second World War, the regimes in Germany and Japan had become ideological machines that threatened the stability of the entire world. In Germany, Hitler's totalitarian state mobilized the nation under the creed of racial supremacy. Every institution—schools, media, courts, even churches—was bent into the service of the Nazi worldview. Dissent was crushed through the Gestapo and the SS. Millions were enslaved as forced laborers, while Jews, Roma, the disabled, and political opponents were marked for extermination in an industrial genocide that culminated in the Holocaust. The war itself was framed as a war of annihilation: entire populations in Eastern Europe were targeted for enslavement or eradication in pursuit of the Nazi vision of *Lebensraum*.[1]

Japan followed a different but equally destructive path. The state fused emperor worship with militant nationalism, demanding absolute loyalty and sacrifice. The cult of the divine emperor justified imperial conquest across Asia, while the Bushidō ethic was weaponized to sanctify death in battle. Surrender was taught to be dishonorable; death for the emperor was glorified as the highest virtue. This fanaticism gave rise to the infamous kamikaze pilots, young men ordered to crash their planes into American ships, and suicidal banzai charges that wasted thousands of lives in hopeless assaults.

What made these regimes so dangerous was the fact that millions embraced them as if they were divine missions. In Germany, Hitler was not merely a political leader; he was exalted as the *Führer,* the embodiment of the nation's destiny. His words carried the weight of scripture and were endlessly preached through rallies, broadcasts, and propaganda that blurred the line between politics and liturgy. The Nazi Party created rituals—torchlight parades, salutes, mass rallies at Nuremberg—that functioned like sacred ceremonies, binding the people into a cult of blood and soil. Children were indoctrinated from the earliest age in the Hitler Youth, taught that to die for the Reich was the highest honor.

Japan mirrored this same religious intensity in its own form. The emperor was not a politician but a living god, the divine descendant of the sun goddess Amaterasu. His commands were treated as sacred edicts, and loyalty to him was loyalty to heaven itself. Both systems were, in essence, political religions.

When the Allies finally broke the military power of Germany and Japan, they did more than conquer armies and topple governments—they humiliated the gods themselves. In Germany, Hitler's suicide in a Berlin bunker shattered the illusion of the *Führer* as an invincible prophet. The Reich he had promised would last a thousand years lay in ashes after barely twelve. Concentration camps were liberated, and the sacred mission of the Aryan race collapsed into the undeniable reality of gas chambers and mass graves. The god of Nazism had failed, and the religion of racial destiny was exposed as a cult of death.

In Japan, the defeat was even more dramatic. The emperor was forced by the Americans to renounce his divinity publicly.[2] The god of the Japanese people became just a man. Hiroshima and Nagasaki obliterated not only two cities but also the myth of divine protection and invincibility. The Bushidō-fueled dream of imperial destiny ended in surrender, and the same soldiers who had once sworn to die for the emperor now watched him bow to the will of foreign occupiers. The sacred aura that had justified conquest, martyrdom, and mass sacrifice was stripped away in an instant.

Within a single generation after their defeat, both Germany and Japan rose from devastation to become stable, prosperous democracies. In Germany, the rubble of the Third Reich gave way to the *Wirtschaftswunder,* the "economic miracle." Factories opened, industries modernized, and within decades, West Germany had become one of the leading economies of the world. At the same time, democratic institutions took root: multiparty elections, a strong rule of law, and checks on state power. The same nation that had once waged total war on Europe was now a reliable partner in peace and a cornerstone of the Western alliance.

Japan underwent a parallel transformation. Under American occupation, its feudal-style militarism was dismantled, and a new constitution enshrined parliamentary democracy, civil rights, and limits on state power. Far from returning to conquest, Japan poured its energy into technological advancement, trade, and education. By the 1960s and 1970s, Japan had become an economic powerhouse, exporting innovation and culture around the globe.

When America invaded Afghanistan in 2001 and Iraq in 2003, it did so with the confidence of a nation that had already proven it could remake shattered societies. The memory of Germany and Japan loomed large in the minds of policymakers. Twice in the 20th century, the United States had not only defeated violent totalitarian regimes but had rebuilt those nations into thriving, democratic allies. Germany and Japan had gone from enemies bent on global domination to pillars of the free world. South Korea, too, had emerged from the chaos of war into prosperity and democracy. Washington assumed Iraq and Afghanistan could follow the same trajectory.

The reasoning seemed straightforward. These countries, like Germany and Japan, were ruled by brutal regimes that had terrorized their people and threatened global security. Saddam Hussein's Iraq was a police state marked by mass graves, chemical attacks, expansion, and a cult of personality. Afghanistan under the Taliban was a medieval theocracy that harbored terrorists and crushed women under rigid oppression. To American leaders, the situation looked familiar: remove the dictators, topple the regime, and then introduce democratic institutions, free markets, and constitutional limits. With sufficient aid and oversight, the people, freed from tyranny, would naturally embrace liberty and prosperity.

But the American project in Iraq and Afghanistan collapsed into catastrophe. Trillions of dollars were spent, thousands of American lives were lost, and yet the results were the opposite of what Washington envisioned. In Iraq, the fall of Saddam Hussein unleashed a wave of sectarian bloodshed. Shia militias, empowered by newfound dominance, sought revenge and control under the guidance of clerics. Sunnis, stripped of the power they had held for decades, turned to insurgency, eventually fueling Al-Qaeda in Iraq and later the rise of ISIS, the most brutal jihadist movement of the 21st century.

Afghanistan followed an equally devastating trajectory. When U.S. troops withdrew in 2021, the entire system the U.S. built collapsed in mere days. The Taliban returned to Kabul without resistance, reclaiming the very power they had lost twenty years earlier. Instead of producing stable allies, the interventions left behind shattered states and emboldened enemies. In Iraq, America unintentionally created the conditions for Iran's expansion and ISIS's rise. In Afghanistan, it fought the longest war in American history only to see the country fall back into the hands of the very regime it had overthrown.

Why did America succeed in Japan and Germany but fail in Iraq and Afghanistan?

The ideologies that dragged Germany and Japan into destruction were powerful, but they were ultimately state-driven constructs—manufactured, amplified, and enforced to unify the nation around a central figure. Both systems functioned like religions, but religions bound to mortal men. Their rituals, their scriptures, their claims to truth, all orbited around a single earthly center. And when those figures fell, the ideologies fell with them. Once the central pillars were broken, the systems they upheld collapsed, leaving a vacuum that could be filled by a new order. This was why democratic institutions and market reforms could take root so quickly: the old gods were dead, and the people were freed from their spell.

But Iraq and Afghanistan were not ruled by a passing ideology or the charisma of a single ruler. Neither Saddam Hussein nor the Taliban was the true god of those societies. The god of Iraq and Afghanistan was Allah—transcendent, untouchable, and eternal. When Saddam swung from the gallows, the faith that ordered life in Iraq remained intact. When the Taliban were driven from Kabul, the theological soil that sustained them was not uprooted. Unlike Hitler or Hirohito, Allah could not be killed, dethroned, or humiliated. This god was the absolute sovereign in the Muslim imagination. And His sovereignty stood in direct contradiction to everything America hoped to impose.

THE GLOBALIZATION OF CHRISTIAN ETHICS

Whether in Germany and Japan or in Iraq and Afghanistan, the United States sought to export the very system that had yielded liberty, prosperity, and stability at home—a system built on democratic institutions, free markets, and constitutional limits. The logic seemed straightforward: if this system had birthed the American order, why should it not be universally applicable, capable of rebuilding other shattered nations? This is not to sanitize America's self-interest or its ambition to secure allies; such motives are part of human nature. Yet what critics denounced as "American imperialism" was, in reality, the engine that turned devastated nations into stable, prosperous allies.

But what America was exporting was never merely a political arrangement. It was an ethical system. The institutions—parliaments, constitutions, markets—were only the outer shell. At their core was a moral framework shaped by centuries of Christian thought: a vision of law, labor, and liberty ordered toward human flourishing. What America carried abroad was not just governance; it was a way of understanding man, power, and society. Christianity had always been concerned with life, and life abundant. Its moral law was ordered toward the good of man: *"I came so that you may have life, and have it abundantly"* (John 10:10).

Over centuries, this theological conviction was translated into concrete institutions. Augustine's vision of the two cities, Aquinas's doctrine of natural law, Locke's contract theory, and the Protestant work ethic all became building blocks of Western civilization. Power was limited because man was sinful. Labor was dignified because man was made in God's image. Property and covenant were respected because stewardship was a moral duty. Even the state itself was justified only insofar as it served justice and human flourishing. Church and state were separated in accordance with Christ's command: *"Render unto Caesar the things that are Caesar's, and unto God the things that are God's"* (Matthew 22:21). This separation was not an act of secular rebellion but the natural fulfillment of Christian teaching.

Over time, these Christian ethics became cloaked in secular, humanistic language. As Western civilization matured, Christian ethics were recast in universal terms that transcended explicit theology. The Enlightenment's language of "natural rights" and "social contracts" was, in truth, the secularized continuation of the Christian vision. Over time, this moral framework was globalized and woven into international charters and institutions. The *Universal Declaration of Human Rights*, for example, enshrines principles that make little sense apart from the Judeo-Christian inheritance: the inherent dignity of the individual, the sanctity of life, and the moral obligation of rulers to serve justice. Nations aspiring to join the modern world could not escape adopting this moral grammar born of Christianity. Whether in constitutions, treaties, or global organizations, the ethical DNA of Christianity, repackaged in secular humanist language, became the assumed foundation of what it meant to be "civilized."

Postwar nation-building did not require mass conversion to Christianity in order to yield similar outcomes. What mattered was whether a society's theological soil was compatible with Christian ethics. In Germany, that soil was already present. For centuries, Christian thought had shaped German life, and even under the darkness of Nazism, voices like Dietrich Bonhoeffer reminded the nation of its true foundation. His resistance to Hitler and his theology of costly discipleship embodied a Christian ethic that could not be extinguished. When Hitler fell, Germany did not need to invent a new moral order; it returned to one it had long known. Repentance from Nazism meant rediscovering its Christian inheritance, which allowed democracy, human rights, and rule of law to take root quickly and endure.

Japan, though not historically Christian, possessed cultural and ethical traditions that did not resist Western institutions. The collapse of State Shintō and the emperor cult created a vacuum into which democratic ideals could enter. Japan was able to adapt to constitutional democracy and free markets without a theological clash. While Christianity remained a minority faith, the society proved compatible enough with Judeo-Christian principles of law, rights, and civic order for the system to flourish.

UNIVERSALIZATION OF JUDAISM

The moral framework that shaped Western civilization through Christianity does not begin with Christianity itself —it begins with Israel. Christianity did not create a new ethic out of thin air. It inherited one. At its deepest roots, what we call *Judeo-Christian morality* comes from the covenantal life of Israel with God. Christianity simply took that covenantal framework and extended it to the whole world.

At the heart of Judaism lies something radically different from every other ancient religion: a God who is personal and relational. The pagan gods of the surrounding nations demanded appeasement. They had to be manipulated, bargained with, or feared. But the God of Israel was different. He entered into covenant: *"I am the Lord your God, who brought you out of Egypt"* (Exodus 20:2). Only after this declaration of redemption does the giving of the law begin. Notice the order: redemption comes first, law comes after. In other words, obedience is never about earning God's favor. It is always a response to God's grace. That is a relational ethic, not a transactional one. Christianity inherits this and then deepens it. The incarnation is the ultimate fulfillment of God's nearness: *"The Word became flesh and dwelt among us"* (John 1:14). The tabernacle presence in the wilderness became flesh-and-blood presence in Christ. So when Jesus says, *"Love one another as I have loved you"* (John 13:34), He is not introducing a brand-new morality. He is showing what the Law and the Prophets were always aiming toward: holiness as the imitation of the God who first loved us.

Judaism also gave the world a revolutionary view of human dignity and responsibility. Unlike pagan fatalism, the Torah presents every human as endowed with the ability—and the responsibility—to choose: *"See, I have set before you today life and death, blessings and curses. Now choose life"* (Deuteronomy 30:19). Human beings are not cogs in a cosmic machine; they are moral agents accountable before God. Christianity universalizes this even further. What Israel was told about being a *"kingdom of priests"* (Exodus 19:6), the New Testament applies to all believers: *"You are a chosen people, a royal priesthood"* (1 Peter 2:9). That means every believer, regardless of birth or station, carries moral responsibility and dignity before God. From this soil grew modern ideas of equality and universal rights.

Judaism also brought history into ethics. In the pagan world, time was cyclical, empires rose and fell endlessly. But Israel's prophets insisted that history is going somewhere. God is moving it toward justice, renewal, and restoration. That's why the prophets didn't just preach ritual purity; they thundered about justice: *"Let justice roll down like waters"* (Amos 5:24). Their vision was always forward-looking, eschatological, awaiting a new heaven, a new earth, a new covenant (Isaiah 65:17; Jeremiah 31:31). Christianity takes up this eschatological hope and centers it in Christ. *"The Kingdom of God has come"* (Mark 1:15), Jesus declared. It is already here in seed form, though not yet fully consummated. That dual reality—already and not yet—gives Christian ethics both urgency and patience: urgency, because the Kingdom has broken in; patience, because its fullness is still to come.

And crucially, Judaism's particularity—its covenant with one people—was never meant to remain particular. The promise to Abraham was that *"through you all nations on earth will be blessed"* (Genesis 12:3). Isaiah foresaw a time when *"all nations will stream to the mountain of the Lord"* (Isaiah 2:2–3). Christianity is not a departure from that universal promise; it is its fulfillment. The Great Commission—*"Go and make disciples of all nations"* (Matthew 28:19) —is the natural outflow of the Abrahamic covenant.

The Judeo-Christian ethic is not two separate traditions artificially stitched together. It is one story, one covenantal thread. It begins with Israel's God, revealed in covenant, law, and prophecy. It comes to fullness in Christ, who universalizes that covenant and carries it to the nations. And from that root grew the moral architecture of the modern West: law, liberty, equality, and justice.

THE ABRAHAMIC RELIGIONS

Imagine two people discussing *The Godfather*. One has seen only Part I, where Marlon Brando is the Godfather. The other has seen both Part I and Part II, where Robert De Niro also portrays the Godfather in his youth. It is possible for the first person to deny that De Niro is the same Godfather, but his denial does not invalidate the deeper knowledge of the second viewer. Both are referring to the same character, just at different points in the story.

This is the relationship between Judaism and Christianity. The Jews do not recognize Jesus as the incarnate God of Israel (John 1:14), yet that does not mean Christians worship a different God. Both Jews and Christians share the same God of Abraham, Isaac, and Jacob (Exodus 3:6; Matthew 22:32). They affirm the same Scriptures, the same Psalms, the same prophets, the same divine attributes, and the same covenantal faithfulness. Christianity did not hijack Israel's story; it embraced and fulfilled it. Where Judaism saw God's promises in shadow, Christianity sees their substance in Christ (Hebrews 10:1).

Christians believe it was the God of Israel who planted Melchizedek into the narrative of Genesis 14:18–20 so that when Jesus claimed priesthood "in the order of Melchizedek" (Hebrews 7:17), His claim would be validated outside the Levitical line. It was the God of Israel who commanded Abraham to offer up Isaac (Genesis 22:1–19), having Isaac carry the wood up Mount Moriah, a foreshadowing of God the Father offering His own Son, carrying the cross up the hill of Calvary (John 19:17). It was the God of Israel who walked through the pieces of the covenant sacrifice after putting Abraham to sleep (Genesis 15:17), and it was the same God who fulfilled that covenant in Christ's death, being slaughtered on behalf of Abraham's descendants (Galatians 3:16).

Christianity holds the highest possible view of the Law of God. The Torah was given to reveal sin and our inability to save ourselves (Romans 3:20; Galatians 3:24). Before the Law, between Adam and Moses, death reigned (Romans 5:14). After the Law, death still reigned, so that humanity might recognize its need for a Savior. Both Jews and Christians participate in God's mission of *tikkun olam*, healing the world and ushering in His eternal kingdom (Isaiah 49:6; Revelation 21:1–4).

This shared narrative is a deliberate, divine orchestration that pulses with purpose and coherence. The God of Israel is not a fragmented deity but a singular, sovereign architect who weaves every detail, Abraham's covenant, Moses' Law, David's throne, and the prophets' cries, into a relentless story of redemption. From Genesis to Revelation, the Scriptures unfold a unified vision where God's character is unchanging, His covenants unbreakable, and His pursuit of humanity unwavering. Judaism holds the roots, Christianity the branches, yet both are grafted into the same tree of God's eternal plan. In this unity we see the epic of divine love that binds them. This covenantal storyline, rooted in the God of Abraham, is what sets the Judeo-Christian faith apart as a singular, unshakable testimony to a God who acts in history to redeem His people.

Now, imagine you've never seen *The Shawshank Redemption*. You don't know Andy Dufresne, you don't know the story of hope carved slowly out of despair, you don't know the weight of the biblical imagery of a man crawling through filth into freedom. Instead, the only exposure you've had are a handful of parody sketches on *Saturday Night Live*. They exist—actors playing prison guards, Andy tunneling through papier-mâché walls, a punchline about Rita Hayworth posters. You'd see the same names, the same prison bars, the same crude imitations of scenes. But if you watched a thousand sketches, however artistically staged, you would still never grasp the soul of *Shawshank*. You'd never feel the arc of redemption, the gravity of justice and mercy, or the theme of ultimate liberation.

This is the relationship between Islam and the Abrahamic faiths of Judaism and Christianity. Islam borrows the names, some concepts, and the surface details, but it fails to deliver the substance. It invokes the God of the Bible as if He were the same deity, but it completely misrepresents His character, His covenant, and His purposes. Islam borrows the names but empties them of their true identity. It infuses them with a foreign vision that has no organic connection to Israel's story. The God of Islam seems to have no understanding of covenant, no sense of why God sent prophets in the first place, no recognition of the meaning behind the Law, the concept of atonement, the Tabernacle, the Temple, the Exile, or the coming of the Messiah. It misses entirely why Jesus came, who He was, and what He accomplished.

The Qur'an even confuses details of biblical stories, blending together Haman (an official in the Persian court, Esther 3:1) with Pharaoh's minister (Qur'an 28:6), a clear historical incoherence. This is why Islam cannot be considered an Abrahamic religion. It not only fractures the biblical narrative but also presents a vision of God and ethics antithetical to the God of Scripture.

The God of Israel promises Himself as the ultimate reward (Genesis 15:1; Psalm 73:25). The God of the Qur'an promises sensual delights, "companions with large breasts and beautiful eyes" (Qur'an 44:54; 52:20). The God of Israel calls His people to holiness because He is holy (Leviticus 19:2; 1 Peter 1:16). The Qur'an's Allah demands submission (*islām*) above all else, regardless of inner transformation (Qur'an 4:65). The God of the Bible works through covenant and redemption. The Qur'an offers no redemption, only scales of deeds weighed on Judgment Day (Qur'an 23:102–103). The God of Scripture does not delight in judgment but desires repentance (Ezekiel 18:23). The Qur'an's Allah declares His will to "fill Hell with jinn and men" (Qur'an 32:13).

The Qur'an portrays Allah as strangely preoccupied with Muhammad's personal affairs: defending Aisha in 18 verses against rumors of infidelity (Qur'an 24:11–20), threatening Muhammad's wives for their discontent (Qur'an 33:30–31), and justifying Muhammad's marriage to Zayd's former wife (Qur'an 33:37). Meanwhile, the Qur'an gives no coherent explanation of Jewish or Christian doctrine. It levels false accusations against Jews, claiming that they worship Uzair (Ezra) as the "son of God" (Qur'an 9:30). It goes so far as to accuse God of manipulating history itself, claiming that Jesus was not crucified but that someone else was made to look like Him, thereby misleading the entire world (Qur'an 4:157).

It then compounds the distortion by misrepresenting

the central Christian confession of the Trinity, reducing it to a crude parody in which Christians supposedly worship God, Mary, and Jesus together (Qur'an 4:171; cf. 5:116), a misunderstanding completely alien to the biblical doctrine of Father, Son, and Holy Spirit. Even in eschatology, Islam diverges radically. Judaism looks for the Messiah to bring peace and restoration (Isaiah 11:1–9). Christianity proclaims Christ's return to renew creation (Revelation 21:1–4). Islam, however, envisions Jesus returning not to redeem but to "break the cross and kill the pigs" (Sahih al-Bukhari 2222; Sahih Muslim 155), waging war rather than bringing healing.

Thus, the Judeo-Christian narrative stands as a towering, unified edifice of divine revelation, its foundations sunk deep in the history of Israel and its capstone set in the person of Christ. Islam, despite its claims, builds on a different foundation, one that cannot bear the weight of the biblical story's depth, complexity, or redemptive power. The God of Abraham calls His people to a living relationship, a journey toward holiness and eternal communion. This call, vibrant and unbroken across millennia, remains the heartbeat of the Abrahamic faith, a legacy that endures in Judaism and Christianity alone.

INSPIRATION VS. DICTATION

The Qur'an does not stand in the same relation to Muslims as the Tanakh to Jews or the New Testament to Christians. The Jewish and Christian Scriptures are divinely inspired but never reduced to mechanical dictation. They were written through men who bore their own voices, contexts, and personalities. (2 Peter 1:21, Hebrews 1:1, 2 Samuel 23:2). What emerges is a canon profoundly human in voice yet unmistakably divine in origin. Inspiration means God's Word entered history through human agents.

By contrast, the Qur'an is not thought of as inspired through human voices at all, but as Allah's unmediated speech, dictated verbatim to Muhammad through Gabriel. It is uncreated and eternal. Just as Allah is eternally knowing and eternally powerful, he is eternally speaking, and the Qur'an is that eternal speech. For this reason Sunni Muslims swear oaths upon the book itself, convinced that it does not merely contain God's word but is God's word in essence: an attribute of Allah deposited in ink and paper (*mushaf*).

The closest Christian parallel is not Scripture but Christ Himself: "In the beginning was the Word, and the Word was with God, and the Word was God... and the Word became flesh" (John 1:1, 14). In Christianity, God's eternal Word is a Person, the Son. In Islam, the eternal Word is not incarnate in flesh but crystallized in a book. One is relational and personal, the other textual and impersonal.

The Jewish and Christian Bibles emerged over centuries, bearing the fingerprints of exile, lament, prophecy, war, vision, and pastoral care. The Tanakh took shape across a millennium, penned by dozens of authors — Moses, the prophets, the psalmists. The New Testament was written within a single century by apostles and their companions. Altogether, the canon reflects some forty authors over fifteen centuries. Each brings distinct vocabulary, genre, and perspective, yet all converge upon a single theocentric vision.

This dynamic made Judaism and Christianity not merely religions of the book but religions of interpretation. God's word invites wrestling. Jacob's night struggle at the Jabbok (Genesis 32:22–32) becomes emblematic of the faithful posture toward revelation: not passive receipt, but engagement. Hence the Talmud in Judaism, centuries of commentary and councils in Christianity, the endless debates of rabbis and church fathers — diversity of voices generating theology, law, science, and philosophy.

The Qur'an, by contrast, was recited to one man over a single lifetime. It presents itself as perfect, beyond history, untouchable by human fingerprints. To question it is to question Allah himself. Hence the highest intellectual activity in Islam is not interpretation but repetition: recitation (*tajwīd*), memorization (*ḥifẓ*), imitation of Muhammad's life. Where Jews could debate *halakha*, and Christians argue Christology, Muslims are told that the only authentic hermeneutic is Muhammad's biography. His actions and words form the key by which every verse must be read. This is why Islamic law freezes itself in the seventh century: to interpret is to replicate Muhammad, nothing more.

This divergence spills directly into how each faith views man and his freedom before God. By speaking through human voices, the God of Israel dignified human agency. The covenant is always relational: God calls, man responds.

> "I have set before you life and death, blessing and curse. Therefore choose life" (Deuteronomy 30:19).

I remember watching a show where a Jewish son told his father, "I joined Jews for Jesus." The father laughed. As a teenager in Jordan, I could never have imagined such a scene in a Muslim family. A son announcing, "I joined Muslims for Buddha," would not draw laughter but rage, shame, and violence. Later, living in Lebanon, I saw Christians convert to Islam or even embrace atheism, and still live with their families, arguing at dinner tables but not being cast out or killed. That kind of freedom is unimaginable in Islam. The reason lies in the very structure of authority. If the Qur'an is Allah's eternal speech, rejecting Islam is not a personal decision but treason against God's very essence. This is why Islamic law prescribes death for apostasy. The hadith says: "Whoever changes his religion, kill him" (Sahih al-Bukhari 3017). Apostasy (*ridda*) is rebellion, not conscience.

Muslims often point to this contrast and use it as a proof of superiority. To them, the ease with which Jews and Christians may leave their faith proves those religions are weak, corrupted, not binding. But in reality, this exposes the very chasm we are describing. The God of Israel seeks covenant partners, not coerced slaves. He invites worshippers who respond in love. The Allah of the Qur'an demands submission under threat of death. One tradition generates fathers who laugh, families who argue yet embrace; the other generates systems where laughter cannot coexist with dissent, only rage and fear.

MIRAGE OF MORALITY

In a recent interview, Tucker Carlson mocked critics of Sharia law by comparing two cities: Dubai and Baltimore. *Look at Dubai,* he said—it is safe, prosperous, and orderly. *Look at Baltimore*—chaos, crime, and decay.[3] The insinuation was that if Islam produces Dubai and secular liberalism produces Baltimore, then perhaps we should not fear Islam.

Tucker did not invent this line of argument. He absorbed it from Muslims themselves. For decades, Muslims have pointed to the West's visible sins—pornography, prostitution, drugs, broken families, LGBT movements, crime rates—and contrasted them with the apparent order of Muslim societies. *"Your freedom creates decadence,"* they say. *"Our Islam produces morality."* This argument is persuasive precisely because it plays on a real Western anxiety: the fear that liberty has corroded virtue.

But Dubai's "safety" is not the fruit of Islam. It is the product of authoritarian control, fear, and the disposability of human beings. Ninety percent of Dubai's population are foreigners who will never be citizens. They are tolerated only so long as they produce. Dubai is a laboratory city where social contamination is instantly removed. To live in Dubai is to live as a guest in someone else's house, knowing you can be expelled at any moment. You are not free to fail, not free to speak, not free to be human.

Even this controlled environment does not come from Sharia. On the contrary, Dubai can function only because it suspends Sharia. If Islamic law were implemented, the financial system would collapse, the expatriate workforce would flee, and the luxury tourism industry would vanish overnight. The very success Muslims parade before the West is built not on Islamic law but on its neglect. Dubai is not proof that Sharia works. It is proof that Sharia cannot.

Baltimore is messy, flawed, and often violent. Poverty, crime, and broken institutions scar the city. But what exists in Baltimore—what Dubai can never provide—is freedom. In Baltimore, people live as citizens, not as tolerated guests. They can fail and try again. They can protest, speak, publish, and belong regardless of religion, race, or background. In Dubai, the law is valued more than people. In Baltimore, people are valued more than the law. This is why, for all its problems, Baltimore is more human than Dubai will ever be. Baltimore exposes the cost of liberty, but also its dignity. A man in Baltimore may stumble, may even fall into crime or addiction, but he remains a man: free to repent, free to rebuild, free to belong. In Dubai, the same man is disposable, erased from the system the moment he becomes inconvenient.

The Dubai–Baltimore comparison is only one layer in the long list of morality contrasts Muslims like to point at. Another favorite is the objectification of women in the West. They claim Islam is superior because it separates women, covers them, and keeps men from distraction. But if your answer to human desire is to segregate women and throw fabric over them, you haven't elevated the soul —you've just built a cage for it. This exposes the core flaw of Islam: it doesn't change people, it restrains them. It doesn't teach growth, discipline, or responsibility. It doesn't cultivate inner strength. It simply locks everything down, assumes men are uncontrollable animals, assumes women are dangerous bait, and calls that morality.

Islam does not produce morality; it produces suppression. It does not build conscience; it builds fear. It does not nurture upright men and women; it breeds double lives. The vices Muslims condemn in the West are not absent in Muslim societies. They are often more rampant, only hidden behind veils. Pornography consumption rates in Pakistan, Saudi Arabia, and Egypt rank among the world's highest. Homosexual activity thrives in secret.[4] Prostitution flourishes under Islamic camouflage through *mut'ah* (temporary marriage in Shi'ism) and *misyar* (in some Sunni contexts). Islam does not eliminate vice; it only drives it underground. When vice is hidden, it mutates. It corrupts everything around it. A Western teenager who experiments with drugs or sexuality may confront consequences openly, painfully, and publicly. In Islam, the same teenager is forced into denial, silence, or violence. What should be an individual struggle becomes a cultural rot. Hypocrisy ceases to be a personal failing; it becomes the lifeblood of the system. Islamic morality is never authentic. It is a mask worn over the same brokenness that exists everywhere else, only enforced with violence. Without the whip, the illusion of order collapses. True morality does not require violence to sustain itself. Virtue chosen under fear is not virtue at all. It is slavery.

Western freedom, for all its excesses, is still superior to Islamic "morality." Freedom allows sin to be visible, debated, confronted. Islam hides sin until it metastasizes. Freedom treats men and women as moral agents capable of choice, even when those choices are destructive. Islam treats them as slaves (*'abd*), whose worth lies in conformity, not character. This is not to deny the West's moral crisis. Pornography does erode intimacy. The collapse of family life wounds children. Gender ideology distorts nature. But Islam has no solution to these crises. It offers only control: rules, punishments, and shame. It offers no redemption, no healing, no grace. Christian civilization, at its height, showed another way. Not the elimination of sin, but the cultivation of conscience. Not fear, but love. Not slavery, but freedom. Islam does not stand as a fortress of morality. It stands as a monument of fear, a regime of hypocrisy, and a counterfeit of true righteousness.

MARY AND JESUS IN ISLAM

Muslims emphasize that Jesus ('Īsā) is mentioned frequently in the Qur'an, that Mary (Maryam) is honored with an entire chapter named after her, and that Islam acknowledges Jesus as a prophet of God. Superficially, this sounds appealing, especially to uninformed Christians who assume this overlap must represent genuine common ground. But when examined closely, this claim collapses. The Jesus and Mary of the Qur'an are not the biblical figures known to Christians, and they are certainly not honored. They are appropriated, rewritten, and weaponized in order to dismantle the very foundations of Christianity. Islam does not "respect" Jesus. It negates Him. It does not "honor" Mary. It exploits her. Every reference to them in the Qur'an functions not to elevate them but to conscript them into Muhammad's project of replacing Christianity with Islam.

The claim is that Mary is the only woman mentioned by name in the Qur'an, and that an entire surah, Surah Maryam, is named after her. This is held up as proof of esteem. But naming is not the same as honoring. If attaching a name were proof of sanctity, then *Surah al-Baqarah* ("The Cow"), *Surah al-Nahl* ("The Bee"), and *Surah al-Naml* ("The Ant") must also be understood as exaltations of livestock, insects, and pests. Clearly, they are not. The Qur'an uses names as literary markers, not as signs of dignity. Mary's presence in the Qur'an has one function: to serve Islam's polemical purposes. Her virginity is affirmed not to exalt her, but to deny Christ's divine Sonship. Her story is retold not to celebrate her, but to make her testimony endorse Muhammad's theology. She becomes a prop in Islam's denial of the Incarnation.

The Qur'an not only misuses Mary, it also misrepresents her. In Surah 19:28, Mary is addressed as "the sister of Aaron." This is a glaring anachronism. Aaron, the brother of Moses, lived more than a thousand years before Mary, the mother of Jesus. The author of the Qur'an confused Mary (Maryam) with Miriam (the Hebrew name for Moses' sister), collapsing centuries of biblical history into one muddled narrative. Islamic apologists scramble to explain this away, claiming "sister of Aaron" is an honorific title, or that people in her village made a comparison, but the plain reading reveals a fundamental ignorance of Scripture. This blunder shows that the Qur'an's portrayal of Mary does not come from divine revelation but from garbled hearsay of Jewish and Christian traditions circulating in Arabia. The "honor" given to Mary is therefore built on a foundation of distortion.

Even more striking than the misuse of Mary is the Qur'an's treatment of Jesus Himself. Muslims insist that Islam "respects" Jesus because it calls Him a prophet, a messenger, and even *al-Masih* (the Messiah). But these titles are hollowed out, emptied of their biblical meaning, and redefined in ways that directly assault the heart of Christianity. The Qur'an systematically strips Jesus of every identity that makes Him who He is in Christian faith:

- It denies His divinity: *"The Messiah, son of Mary, was only a messenger"* (Qur'an 5:75).
- It denies His Sonship: *"It is not befitting for Allah to take a son"* (Qur'an 19:35).
- It denies His crucifixion: *"They did not kill him, nor crucify him, but it was made to appear so"* (Qur'an 4:157).

In other words, the Qur'an preserves Jesus only in order to negate Him. He is a shell, a name emptied of its substance. The Jesus of Islam is not the eternal Son of God, not the Word made flesh, not the crucified and risen Lord. He is an anti-Jesus, retained only to erase the true one. Islam cannot tolerate the Jesus of the Gospels. If Jesus is divine, Muhammad is irrelevant. If Jesus is the Son of God, Muhammad's message collapses. If Jesus truly died and rose again, then Islam's theology of salvation is a fraud. The Qur'an must therefore silence the real Christ in order to establish Muhammad's authority.

The Qur'an denies the Trinity, the Incarnation, and the Cross—the three pillars of Christian faith. What remains is not Good News but a theological weapon designed to dismantle Christianity at its core. Far from "respecting"

Jesus, the Qur'an makes Him the chief casualty in Islam's war against the Gospel.

The Qur'an does not simply reject the crucifixion; it claims Allah deliberately deceived the world about it. Christians, it says, only thought Jesus was crucified because Allah made it appear so. The Qur'an even calls Allah *khayr al-makireen*, "the best of deceivers" (3:54). By this logic, billions of Christians across history were not merely wrong; they were victims of a divine hoax.

The Qur'an's distortion of Jesus extends beyond the past into the future. Islam teaches that Jesus will return at the end of time. But in Islam's eschatology, His role is not to redeem the world. Instead, He returns to enforce Islam. Jesus returns not as Savior but as Muhammad's enforcer, abolishing Christianity, destroying its symbols, and submitting the world to Sharia.

THE SANITIZED QUR'AN

Most Western readers will never learn Arabic, which means their only encounter with the Qur'an and Hadith comes through English translations. But those translations are not neutral. They are carefully curated, softened, and massaged to produce a marketable version of Islam—an Islam that looks humane, tolerant, and universal. The raw Arabic, however, tells a very different story.

Take one of Muhammad's most oft-quoted sayings: "The Muslim is the one from whose tongue and hand other Muslims are safe." The meaning is blunt. Safety is extended only to Muslims. Non-Muslims are excluded from the circle of moral concern. Yet in Western-friendly versions, the wording is subtly changed: "The Muslim is the one from whose tongue and hand other people are safe." One word is swapped—*Muslims* becomes *people*—and suddenly the hadith reads like a universal ethic of peace. But the original is exclusive.

Qur'an 8:55. Most English editions render it: "Indeed, the worst of living creatures in the sight of Allah are those who disbelieve…" That sounds harsh but still metaphorical. In Arabic, though, the word is al-dawābb (الدَّوَابّ)—a term used for animals, livestock, vermin, crawling things. Disbelievers are not "living creatures" in some neutral sense. They are dehumanized, reduced to the level of beasts of burden and pests. Translators soften the insult because they know if Westerners read the unvarnished Arabic—calling Jews, Christians, and all unbelievers cattle and crawling animals—they would recoil.

Qur'an 9:29, the foundation of Islamic jihad against Jews and Christians. In Arabic it commands: "Fight those who do not believe in Allah or in the Last Day… until they pay the jizya with willing submission and feel themselves humiliated." But Western editions routinely soften the ending: "…until they pay the tax with a willing hand, being humbled." *Humbled* sounds almost dignified, like a mild concession. The Arabic word, however—ṣāghirūn (صاغرون)—is far harsher. It denotes abasement, humiliation, enforced degradation. Classical jurists were explicit: Jews and Christians were to be struck on the neck as they paid the tax, forced to approach in rags, made to feel small. None of this survives the English laundering.

The same tactic appears in Qur'an 5:51: "O you who believe, do not take the Jews and Christians as allies (awliya). They are allies of one another. Whoever among you takes them as allies is one of them." The Arabic *awliya* encompasses friendship, loyalty, alliance. It forbids Muslims from forging bonds with Jews and Christians. Yet Western-friendly translations render *awliya* as "protectors" or "guardians," restricting the verse to a technical political rule. The social and relational ban is erased.

Even the infamous "Sword Verse" (Qur'an 9:5) is subjected to this sanitization. The Arabic command is unequivocal: "Kill the polytheists wherever you find them, capture them, besiege them, and lie in wait for them at every ambush." But some Western printings insert qualifiers that do not exist in the text: *"in battle"* or *"in war."* These additions make the verse sound defensive, as if it applies only to military conflict. But the Arabic is absolute: kill them wherever you find them. No conditions.

This process creates a kind of *parallel Qur'an*—not the Qur'an of Medina, but the Qur'an of public relations. In Muslim-majority societies where Arabic is known, the meaning is obvious and unapologetic. But in the West, where Islam seeks legitimacy as a minority religion, the message must be adapted. And so the sharp edges are filed down for foreign consumption. Muslims themselves will often say, "You must read it in Arabic to truly understand." On one level, this is true. But it is also a trap: most Westerners will never learn Arabic, leaving the gatekeepers in control of the narrative.

Nowhere is this strategy clearer than in the treatment of the word jihad. In every Islamic English translation of the Qur'an, *jihad* disappears. It is never transliterated, as words like *hajj*, *zakat*, or *sharia* are. Instead, translators replace it with vague English equivalents—"fight," "struggle," "strive," "exert effort." This dilution allows apologists to repackage jihad for Western ears: "Oh, jihad just means an inner struggle... resisting temptation... being a better person." But this is not how the Qur'an uses the word, nor how Muslims have ever understood it. In almost every Qur'anic context, jihad is martial. It refers to armed conflict, preparation for war, or financial and material support of fighting. It is outward, militant, always aimed at advancing Islam.

- Surah al-Baqarah 2:216 declares, *"Fighting (qital) has been prescribed for you, even though it is hateful to you..."* Just two verses later, in 2:218, it adds, *"Indeed, those who believed and emigrated and performed jihad in the path of Allah—they hope for Allah's mercy."* Here the meaning of *jihad* is defined by the immediate context: it is the fighting (qital) just prescribed, not a vague inner struggle, but armed conflict undertaken for the cause of Islam.
- Surah Aal Imran 3:142 says, *"Do you think you will enter Paradise while Allah has not yet made evident those of you who perform jihad?"* To understand what this jihad is, the preceding verse (3:141) provides the explanation: *"...that Allah may purge the believers and destroy the disbelievers."* In other words, jihad here is not personal self-improvement—it is the violent process by which believers are "purified" through battle and disbelievers are eliminated.

- Surah an-Nisa 4:95: "Not equal are those believers who sit [at home]... and the mujahideen who perform jihad in the path of Allah with their wealth and their lives..." The distinction is between those who fight and those who refuse.
- Surah at-Tawbah 9:20: "Those who believe, who emigrated, and who performed jihad with their wealth and their lives are greater in rank..."
- Surah at-Tawbah 9:41: "Go forth, whether light or heavy, and perform jihad with your wealth and your lives in the cause of Allah."
- Surah at-Tawbah 9:73: "O Prophet, perform jihad against the disbelievers and the hypocrites and be harsh with them."
- Surah as-Saff 61:11: "You believe in Allah and His Messenger and perform jihad in the cause of Allah with your wealth and your lives..."

Islam in English is staged as if it belongs within the Abrahamic family—just another expression of the one God of Israel, a sibling faith to Judaism and Christianity, sharing their moral heritage and covenantal vision. But the Arabic will not permit such a fiction. The Qur'an in its own language is not a continuation of Israel's story but a rupture. The raw text insists on hierarchy—Muslims above, unbelievers below—and no amount of linguistic laundering can erase that reality.

THE FALSE SEAT AT ABRAHAM'S TABLE

Jews have long been told that Islam is their sibling faith, that its monotheism mirrors their own, and that Christianity—with its Messiah and its Trinity—is the true outlier. This is false. Islam's structure is not a continuation of Judaism's radical monotheism but its undoing. It enthrones a man beside God, and in doing so it drifts further from the Shema* than Judaism ever imagined Christianity did. I am not entering here into a full defense of Christian monotheism. That is not because it lacks an answer. Christianity has always confessed one God—the God of Abraham, Isaac, and Jacob—and the case for its monotheism can certainly be made. But this is not the book for that argument.

My concern here is to expose the dangerous illusion that the real chasm lies between Judaism and Christianity —an illusion believed not only by many Jews but also by many Christians, who imagine that Islam, by revering Jesus, stands closer to them than the Jews who rejected Him.

Judaism and Christianity may differ on the identity of the Messiah, but they share infinitely more than what divides them. Both confess the same God—the One who called Abraham, delivered Israel from Egypt, spoke at

---

* **Shema:** from the Hebrew word *shema* meaning "hear" or "listen." It refers to the central confession of Jewish faith found in Deuteronomy 6:4–5: *"Hear, O Israel: The Lord our God, the Lord is one. Love the Lord your God with all your heart and with all your soul and with all your strength."* The Shema is recited daily in Jewish prayer and affirms the unity of God and Israel's covenant loyalty to Him.

Sinai, and sent the prophets. Both affirm the covenant, the law, and the hope of redemption. Their disagreement is real, but it takes place within the same story, inside the same moral universe, shaped by the same Creator and Judge. Christianity does not replace Israel; it grows out of it. Its roots are Jewish, its Scriptures Jewish, its moral vision Jewish. That is why, despite the break over Christ, Christians and Jews still speak the same theological language, still wrestle with the same history, still stand before the same God.

The god of Islam is not the God of Abraham, Isaac, and Jacob, he does not bear his covenant, he does not share his attributes, and he has no place in his story of promise and redemption. The Lord of Israel binds Himself in covenant love, enters history, and redeems His people. Allah does none of this. He offers no covenant, only command; no redemption, only submission; no Son, only slaves. He does not understand why Abraham was chosen, why Israel was called, why the prophets spoke, why Christ came, or why the cross stands at the center of history. He is foreign to it all—foreign to the Law, foreign to the Prophets, foreign to the Gospel.

Islam's Allah is not another name for the God of the Bible. He is a foreign god, an intruder who borrows Abraham's names but speaks with an alien voice—one who may claim a seat at Abraham's table, but will never belong there.

CHAPTER 6
THE NEW FRONTIERS

POLICY JIHAD

When people think of Islamic expansion, they think of jihad, armies of horsemen storming across deserts, swords raised, banners of Allah flying over conquered cities. But in the twenty-first century, the image is different. The new conquest does not always come with bombs or bullets. It comes with policies, laws, and institutions. It comes dressed in the language of diversity, inclusion, human rights, and multiculturalism.

The old jihad of force has not disappeared—it is still visible in Hamas, Hezbollah, ISIS, Boko Haram, and the Houthis—but it is no longer the only or even the primary mode of expansion in the West. The modern advance of Islam is bureaucratic jihad. It flows through the same global systems that govern finance, health, education, climate, and migration. It rides on the back of what some call the Global Public-Private Partnership (GPPP): the intertwined network of international organizations, central banks, think tanks, corporations, NGOs, governments, and media that sets the agenda for nations.

Islam has learned to play this system. Instead of standing outside it, it infiltrates it. Instead of fighting against the United Nations, it captures UN resolutions. Instead of rejecting Western institutions, it forces those institutions to bend under the weight of accusations of racism, Islamophobia, and colonial guilt. Instead of needing to topple governments, it pressures governments to write laws that censor criticism of Islam, subsidize mosques, and re-engineer education. In short: Islam today expands less through direct jihad than through policy jihad.

If we are serious about defending the West, then we must stop imagining Islamic expansion only in terms of terrorism and violence. We must learn to see how the ideology moves through this system, how it captures each level of policy production and distribution. And most importantly: we must learn how to resist it.

How the Global Policy System Works

The GPPP can be understood as a pyramid of influence. At the top are the policy makers—global banking institutions, central banks, and elite think tanks like the World Economic Forum (WEF), the Council on Foreign Relations (CFR), and Chatham House. These bodies do not merely suggest ideas; they shape the very framework within which governments think about law, economy, and society.

Beneath them are the policy distributors: the United Nations, the World Health Organization, the IMF, the World Bank, NGOs, philanthropists, and global corporations. They take the ideas formulated at the top and spread them globally, embedding them in treaties, conventions, development goals, and corporate standards.

The next level is the policy enforcers: national governments, bureaucracies, courts, military, police, and scientific authorities. This is where the policies are translated into law, regulation, and enforcement on the ground. A UN convention becomes a law passed by Parliament. An IMF condition becomes austerity or restructuring. A WHO guideline becomes national health mandates.

Then come the policy propagandists: the mainstream media, fact-checkers, social media platforms, hybrid warfare specialists, "anti-hate" campaigners. Their task is to make the public believe these policies are moral, scientific, and inevitable. They use censorship, disinformation, and psychological manipulation to shape consent.

Finally, at the bottom, are the policy subjects: the people. Ordinary citizens pay for the system through taxes, are bound by its laws, are pressured by its media narratives, and are punished if they resist.

This is the machinery of global governance. And Islam has figured out how to infiltrate it.

How Islam Expands Through the Policy System
1. At the Policy-Making Level

Islamic governments and lobby groups work closely with the top-tier policy makers. The Organization of Islamic Cooperation (OIC), representing 57 Muslim-majority states, is essentially a parallel United Nations for Islam. It pushes resolutions at the UN to criminalize "Islamophobia" worldwide. It influences think tanks and Western elites through petro-dollars, partnerships, and academic funding. Gulf states pump billions into Western universities, endowing Islamic Studies chairs and think-tanks that subtly reshape policy frameworks.

The result is that the Global elites no longer treat Islam as a religion with problematic doctrines, but as a permanent partner in governance—a culture to be accommodated, protected, and advanced.

2. At the Policy Distribution Level

Through the UN and NGOs, Islam embeds itself into global policy frameworks. UNHCR migration compacts emphasize protecting Muslim refugees, while ignoring the persecution of Christians in Muslim countries. UNESCO rewrites history in Jerusalem to erase Jewish connections and elevate Islamic claims. The WHO and humanitarian NGOs avoid confronting Islamic practices that harm women (FGM, child marriage) for fear of "offending communities." Corporations adopt diversity and inclusion standards that require Islamic accommodations in workplaces, while Christian symbols are banned as "offensive."

3. At the Policy Enforcement Level

National governments are pressured to enforce Islamic sensitivities. Blasphemy laws, long a feature of Islamic states, now creep into the West in the form of "hate speech" laws. Police investigate citizens for criticizing Islam online. Schools teach Islamic history in glowing terms while demonizing Christianity and Judaism. Governments subsidize Islamic organizations in the name of community cohesion, while monitoring and marginalizing groups that expose Islam's ideology.

4. At the Policy Propaganda Level

Media and tech platforms aggressively silence critique

of Islam. Fact-checkers label accurate references to Islamic texts as "misleading." Social media bans voices that expose jihad. Hollywood and streaming services produce endless portrayals of Muslims as victims of prejudice, while erasing the reality of Islamic terrorism. "Anti-hate" campaigners frame any resistance to Islamization as "far-right extremism," creating a chilling effect on public discourse.

5. At the Level of the Public

The result is predictable. Ordinary citizens are conditioned to accept Islam as untouchable. They are taught to apologize for Western history but never to question Islamic history. They are told to see Muslims only as victims, never as aggressors. They are pressured to accept mosque construction, halal mandates, hijab accommodations, and censorship of speech as the price of "diversity." Meanwhile, those who resist are ostracized, fired, fined, or imprisoned.

This is the new jihad: not bombs in the marketplace, but policies in the boardroom. Not swords on the battlefield, but signatures on treaties. Not raids on villages, but regulations in schools. Islam expands by capturing the system that governs the world.

Combating Islamic Expansion at Every Level

If Islam expands through this policy system, then resisting it requires countering it at every level.

1. Combating at the Policy-Making Level

- Expose Islamic Lobbying: Document and publicize how the OIC and Gulf money influence think tanks, universities, and global elites. Transparency destroys the illusion of neutrality.

- Alternative Think Tanks: Build independent Judeo-Christian think tanks that unapologetically defend Western civilization. They must compete directly with WEF and CFR narratives.
- Financial Independence: Push for laws banning foreign funding of academic and political institutions. If Western universities accept Gulf money, they should lose public funding.
- Reframe the Narrative: Constantly hammer the truth that Islam is not a race but an ideology, and must be treated as such at the highest levels of policy-making.

2. Combating at the Policy Distribution Level

- UN Resistance: Western states must veto or withdraw from UN resolutions that criminalize Islamophobia or rewrite history. Support nations that stand against Islamic lobbying.
- NGO Accountability: Demand financial transparency from NGOs and expose Islamic capture. Create alternative NGOs that defend persecuted Christians and Jews, balancing the Islamic narrative.
- Corporate Pushback: Organize shareholder activism against corporations that adopt Islamic accommodation policies while erasing Christian symbols.

3. Combating at the Policy Enforcement Level

- Legislative Clarity: Pass explicit laws protecting freedom of speech on religion. Make it impossible to smuggle Islamic blasphemy laws into hate speech codes.
- End Subsidies: Cut off government funding for Islamic organizations that act as fronts for Muslim Brotherhood or OIC agendas.
- Educational Reform: Reclaim schools from multicul-

tural propaganda. Demand balanced teaching that exposes the reality of Islamic conquest and persecution.

- Law Enforcement Oversight: Hold police accountable for double standards—ignoring Islamic extremism while punishing critics.

4. Combating at the Policy Propaganda Level

- Alternative Media: Invest in platforms that will not censor criticism of Islam. Build news outlets, streaming platforms, and entertainment companies that expose the truth.
- Cultural Counter-Narratives: Produce films, books, and art that tell the stories of those persecuted by Islam—Christians in Nigeria, Druze in Syria, Jews across centuries. Break the monopoly of victimhood.
- Challenge Fact-Checkers: Create fact-checking organizations that expose lies about Islam's peacefulness. Use Islamic texts themselves to show the truth.
- Public Campaigns: Normalize criticism of Islam in the same way criticism of Christianity and Judaism is normalized. Break the taboo through repetition.

5. Combating at the Level of the Public

- Grassroots Movements: Build local resistance against mosque expansion when it functions as ideological beachheads. Mobilize parents against Islamic indoctrination in schools.
- Community Resilience: Strengthen churches and synagogues as counter-institutions to mosques. Encourage unapologetic religious identity as defense against Islamic dominance.
- Demographic Strategy: Encourage strong family structures in the West. Islamic expansion often rides on

demographic advantage. A confident, reproducing West is harder to overrun.

• Civil Courage: Train citizens to speak boldly about Islam, even under pressure. Public courage is contagious. One person resisting gives permission for others to do the same.

From Defense to Offense

The great mistake of the West has been to treat Islam only as a security threat—terrorists, radicals, lone wolves—while ignoring its policy infiltration. But Islam has moved from the battlefield to the boardroom. It does not need to conquer through armies if it can conquer through laws. It does not need suicide bombers if it can recruit lawyers, diplomats, and NGOs.

If the West is to survive, it must learn to fight on this new battlefield. It must recognize that the global policy system has been weaponized against it. And it must reclaim the moral confidence to say: No. No to censorship. No to blasphemy laws. No to erasing crosses from logos. No to Islamic lobbying disguised as diversity.

Combating Islamic expansion is not simply about stopping terrorism. It is about defending civilization from an ideology that has mastered the art of policy capture. The choice before us is stark: either reclaim the system at every level—makers, distributors, enforcers, propagandists—or surrender to slow-motion conquest.

SOVIET ISLAM: THE SECOND BIRTH

In the aftermath of the 1917 Russian Revolution, the Bolsheviks inherited a fractured empire, riddled with ethnic divisions and bound by centuries of religious tradition. Their Marxist creed was built on atheism and class struggle, which meant dismantling religious institutions seen as remnants of the old order. Churches were shuttered or turned into warehouses, synagogues desecrated, and clergy, Christian and Jewish alike, executed or exiled. Their influence was systematically erased. Yet Islam, which dominated Central Asia and the Caucasus, was handled in a different way.

Muslims under Soviet rule were vast in number, geographically dispersed, and deeply tied to their faith. The Bolsheviks knew that outright persecution would ignite uprisings capable of destabilizing their fragile hold on power. Moreover, Islam extended far beyond Soviet borders into British, and French, controlled territories, colonial rivals the Soviets were eager to undermine. As historian Hans Bräker observes, the early Soviet period up to 1927 was marked by a "relatively soft treatment" of Islam. Through policies of korenizatsiya (indigenization), Muslim elites were permitted to retain influence in local administration. At the same time, the Soviets infiltrated mosques and madrasas, engineering what became known as "Soviet Islam," a hollowed-out, state-approved version of the faith. At the 1920 Baku Congress of the Peoples of the East, Bolshevik leaders Zinoviev and Radek even called for a "holy war" (gazavat) against Western imperialism, co-opting Islamic rhetoric to align Muslims with Soviet revolutionary aims.

By the mid-1920s, the state had woven Islam into its machinery of control. Mosques and religious councils were placed under direct oversight, ensuring sermons were infused with Soviet ideology. Muslim figures like Mir-Said Sultan Galiev were elevated to prominence, blending Marxist language with Islamic motifs to appeal to local loyalties. This dual strategy, appropriating Islamic identity at home while exporting it abroad, gave the Bolsheviks a lever of influence far beyond Russia's borders. In the Middle East, where anti-colonial sentiment was on the rise, Soviet-backed Islamic movements provided a convenient proxy against Western powers.

The Seeds of Western Infiltration

The Bolsheviks' exploitation of Islam did not stop with domestic co-optation. They saw in Islam a potential weapon against their geopolitical rivals. Beginning in the 1920s, Moscow encouraged the migration of Muslim refugees into Europe and British and French-controlled regions, deliberately seeding unrest in colonial territories. These refugees were not random wanderers; they were part of a larger Soviet strategy to project instability under the banner of religious identity.

Nowhere was this more evident than in Palestine. Soviet support for anti-colonial causes quickly translated into ideological and material backing for Arab nationalist groups. By the late 1930s, Soviet influence had begun shaping the trajectory of Palestinian activism, setting the stage for organizations like the PLO decades later. When the PLO formally emerged in 1964, its leftist factions, especially George Habash's Popular Front for the Liberation of Palestine (PFLP), were already firmly in the orbit of Moscow. The PFLP embodied the fusion of Marxism and armed struggle, targeting both Western imperialism and secular Arab regimes. High-profile hijackings and acts of terror in the 1960s and 1970s were not random outbursts but calculated maneuvers to internationalize the Palestinian cause while destabilizing Western confidence. Archival evidence shows the PFLP was armed and trained by the KGB, with operatives like Wadie Haddad serving as Soviet intelligence assets.

The Soviet Union had learned that Islam could be manipulated as a vehicle of revolutionary destabilization. It could rally masses under a religious identity while advancing Marxist geopolitical goals.

The Left's Contemporary Playbook

Fast forward to the 21st century, and a strikingly similar dynamic is visible in the West. Radical factions of the political left now align themselves with Islamic causes, presenting them as struggles against capitalism, imperialism, and systemic oppression. The alignment is tactical. As the Bolsheviks once did, today's left sees in Islam a prepackaged identity group that can be weaponized against Western cultural and political foundations.

The pattern is unmistakable. Christianity and Judaism are relentlessly critiqued in progressive discourse, often caricatured as patriarchal or colonial legacies. Yet Islam is spared. Under the protective banner of "multiculturalism," Islam enjoys immunity from the same critique leveled against other religions. Criticism is quickly condemned as "Islamophobia." This selective defense mirrors the Soviet approach, where Islam was shielded because it could be used as an instrument of political leverage.

The immigration policies of Western leftist governments further echo Soviet precedent. Open borders and expansive asylum programs, especially in Europe and North America, have ushered in waves of Muslim migrants who now reshape demographics and cultural dynamics. These policies are justified as humanitarian, but they also import populations resistant to assimilation and primed to challenge Western cohesion. The social tensions that follow, conflicts over crime, integration, or cultural clashes, are then weaponized by the left as evidence of Western racism and oppression, further undermining traditional institutions.

Islam's Unique Immunity

Unlike communism or radical leftist ideologies, Islam is not seen as merely political but as a religion. It wraps itself in that mantle, which in the West carries a unique immunity. Governments may ban a party, censor a movement, or outlaw an ideology, but religion occupies a separate, protected category. Islam exploits this shield. The very protections liberal societies extend to religion, freedom of worship, legal recognition, deference to belief, become barriers against critique or containment.

Communism collapsed under scrutiny when its promises failed. Radical leftism can be contested in the open marketplace of ideas. But Islam advances under cover, immune to exposure, because any honest critique is recast as bigotry. The Bolsheviks understood this a century ago: Islam, precisely because it is religion, could be harnessed with less resistance than their atheistic creed.

Today's radical left has rediscovered the same insight. By allying with Islam, they gain a revolutionary partner that enjoys protections they themselves could never claim.

The PLO and PFLP as Case Studies

The Palestinian Liberation Organization and its Marxist factions serve as a case study in this strategy. The PLO wore the garb of nationalism, but its Marxist wings fused Palestinian identity with Soviet ideology. The PFLP became the poster child of this fusion, carrying out spectacular attacks in the name of liberation while serving Soviet aims. These groups garnered sympathy among Western radicals who saw their struggle as a mirror of their own battles against capitalism and imperialism. Western leftist groups provided propaganda support, fundraising, and even logistical assistance. The PFLP's ties to the Red Army Faction in Germany and the Japanese Red Army show how Islam and Marxism could fuse into an international revolutionary network.

What began as a Soviet tactic has now become a template for today's radical left. Today, this legacy persists in the left's unwavering support for Palestinian causes. The Boycott, Divestment, and Sanctions (BDS) movement, for instance, draws heavily on the rhetoric of anti-imperialism and anti-Zionism, framing Israel as a colonial oppressor while ignoring the Islamic roots of the Israeli-Palestinian conflict.

The Palestinian intellectual Ghassan Kanafani, himself a PFLP leader, described the cultural struggle against the West as a "cultural siege." He understood propaganda as a weapon in war. Today, that same dynamic persists. Islam is used as both shield and sword. Shielded by claims of victimhood and religious privilege, Islam is insulated from scrutiny. Wielded as a sword, its grievances and identity politics are deployed to attack Western culture and delegitimize its moral foundations.

ISRAEL AND THE SOUL OF CONSERVATISM

I am not an American, at least not yet, and I've only been living in the U.S. for two years. Still, it's clear to me that in today's America, defending Israel is inextricably bound to defending the core values that underpin the conservative movement itself: religious liberty, individual responsibility, family integrity, and reverence for Western civilization. When support for Israel falters, that foundation begins to crack.

The correlation between political conservatism and support for Israel is statistical and consistent. According to a Gallup poll released in March 2025,[1] 75 percent of Republicans sympathize more with Israelis in the Middle East conflict, while just 21 percent of Democrats do. In contrast, 59 percent of Democrats express greater sympathy for Palestinians, the highest level ever recorded. This is not a split; it is a chasm. The favorability divide is just as stark. As of April 2025, Pew Research Center data[2] shows that 69 percent of Democrats now hold an unfavorable view of Israel, up from 53 percent in 2022. Among Republicans, only 37 percent view Israel unfavorably, while a majority still view it favorably. Among white evangelical Protestants, who represent the backbone of the conservative grassroots, 72 percent view Israel favorably. In sharp contrast, among the religiously unaffiliated, an overwhelmingly progressive demographic, 69 percent view Israel negatively. These aren't mere policy preferences; they are identity markers.

Support for Israel, then, is an ideological identifier as clear and decisive as views on, for example, the role of government. It functions as a political signal, a proxy for where one stands on a host of related issues. To support Israel is to affirm belief in moral clarity, civilizational inheritance, and national sovereignty. To oppose Israel is to increasingly align with a worldview that sees Western institutions as oppressive, tradition as a tool of oppression, and religious conviction as a threat.

In American politics, there is what might be called the "bundled-values effect." Voters do not engage politics issue by issue; they choose worldviews and vote for people, platforms, and parties that reflect a coherent moral and cultural framework. In this context, support for Israel has become a bundled value, an issue that travels with others and helps define ideological identity.

"Pro-Israel" candidates are rarely just pro-Israel. They are also pro-family values, pro-religious liberty, and pro-limited government. They defend the Constitution, they see America (and the West) as a real value-add to the world, and they speak the language of responsibility rather than grievance. In other words, they speak the language of conservatism.

Opposition to Israel, by contrast, increasingly travels with opposition to those very values. The same political movements that denounce Israel as a colonial power also denounce the American Founding as systemically oppressive. Many of the same voices that accuse Israel of "apartheid" also demand the deconstruction of the nuclear family and the suppression of religious speech in the public square. The same activists who chant "From the River to the Sea!" are marching to dismantle the Judeo-Christian moral order that made America possible.

Those attacking Israel in the American context are not merely concerned about the policies of a foreign government; they are engaged in a much broader campaign: the delegitimization of Western civilization itself. Israel is not isolated in their moral calculus; it is emblematic. It represents tradition, rootedness, strength, religious identity, and the West's refusal to dissolve itself into guilt and self-loathing.

That is why they hate it. And that is why they target it.

"Progressive" strategists understand something many conservatives do not: If you can fracture the relationship between Israel and America, you can destabilize the very coalition that has held back the "progressive" agenda for decades. They don't have to convince conservative voters to become Marxists; they only need to alienate them from the one issue that aligns them instinctively with pro-liberty and pro-order candidates.

Break that link, and the rest unravels. No less, it is working. Among younger evangelicals, support for Israel has dropped dramatically in recent years. In 2018, 75 percent of evangelical adults under 30 supported Israel. By 2021, that number had fallen below 35 percent. This is the result of relentless academic indoctrination, media demonization, and a social climate that portrays Israel as a pariah and any defense of it as complicity in oppression.

The goal is to shift the vote — because when voters shift away from Israel, they also drift toward candidates and parties that oppose the very foundations of conservative policy: religious freedom, parental rights, and moral education. A conservative disillusioned with Israel today may be persuaded to vote for a non-interventionist Democrat tomorrow, only to find themselves supporting a platform that includes the erosion of gender distinctions and hostility to religion. This is not just a loss for Israel; it is a loss for America and the greater West.

The ideological coalition that attacks Israel does not stop at the borders of the Middle East. Its critique extends to the very core of American society. Israel and America are, in their view, twin evils: settler-colonial powers, capitalist oppressors, and religious zealots. They chant "Free Palestine!" with one breath and "Abolish ICE"[1] with the next. They scream about checkpoints in the West Bank and riot over policing in Atlanta. They equate Gaza with Ferguson, the IDF with the New York Police Department, Zionism with whiteness, and Jewish survival with white supremacy.

The attack on Israel is, therefore, a disguised attack on America's moral legitimacy. It is not about borders; it is about narratives. To delegitimize Israel is to prepare the ground for delegitimizing the Constitution, America's founders, the church, and everything conservatives seek to preserve.

And the conservative movement cannot afford to be naïve about this. Supporting Israel is not optional. It is not symbolic. It is essential to the preservation of a coalition that can withstand the ideological onslaught of the modern Left.

For American voters, the choice is now clear. To support Israel is to vote for candidates who believe in the moral legitimacy of the West. It is to side with those who defend religious liberty, parental rights, and free speech. Voting for pro-Israel candidates is not about taking a side in a foreign conflict; it is about taking a side in a domestic war for America's soul.

For policymakers, the message is just as urgent. Israel policy is not a line item; it is a foundation stone. Support for Israel must be linked with a broader conservative legislative agenda: school choice, tax reform, constitutional originalism, defense of conscience rights, and the curtailment of bureaucratic overreach.

Israel can no longer be treated as an isolated talking point in foreign policy platforms; it must be understood and framed as a civilizational ally in the defense of ordered liberty. Abandoning Israel is not just a betrayal of an ally; it is a surrender to the logic of the modern Left. And that surrender will not stop at the borders of Judea and Samaria; it will march straight into the homes, schools, places of worship, and courts of America.

To rebuild and protect the conservative coalition, leaders must reclaim the moral narrative around Israel. They must speak clearly and unapologetically: Israel is not the problem. Israel is the front line. It is a bulwark against Islamic jihad, totalitarianism, and the "progressive" alliance that excuses terrorism while criminalizing Biblical morality.

Religious leaders must teach the covenantal meaning of Israel. Candidates must link Israel support to every major cultural and political fight in America. Commentators must expose the rhetorical tricks used to smear Zionism, while laundering antisemitism and rebranding Islamic jihad. And voters must be reminded: This is not a marginal issue, but a defining one. If conservatives fail to defend Israel, they will soon find they cannot defend themselves.

The modern Left understands this. They know that breaking the link between Israel and conservatism is a precondition for capturing the electorate. They know that if they can portray Israel as morally illegitimate, they will begin to win more of those who defend family values, believe in law and order, and dismantle the very idea of Western identity.

BANNING THE MUSLIM BROTHERHOOD: WHY THE WEST'S APPROACH FALLS SHORT

In Muslim-majority countries like Egypt, Jordan, Saudi Arabia, and the UAE, banning the Muslim Brotherhood isn't about outlawing a single organization, it's about surgically suppressing the political dimension of Islam. These semi-Islamic governments understand Islam as both a religion and a political system, and they realize that the Muslim Brotherhood represents the most coherent expression of Islam's political ambitions. When these regimes ban the Muslim Brotherhood, they're targeting the ideology it embodies. If a new group emerges with the same principles, advocating for sharia, Islamic rule, or a Caliphate, it faces the same fate. The ban isn't just on the Muslim Brotherhood's name or logo; it's on the political vision it represents. In these countries, the state's Islamic legitimacy allows it to enforce this boundary without being accused of attacking Islam itself. New groups can't simply rebrand and operate openly. The ideology is effectively choked off, regardless of the group's name.

In contrast, the West, particularly the U.S., can only ban the Muslim Brotherhood as a specific entity, not the ideology it represents. Western legal systems, rooted in freedoms of religion and speech, treat Islam as a protected religion, akin to Christianity or Judaism. The Muslim Brotherhood's political goals, grounded in Islamic texts, are seen as expressions of religious belief, not a distinct political ideology. If the West bans the Muslim Brotherhood, new groups with identical aims, sharia advocacy, Islamic governance, can form under different names, such as "cultural societies" or "civil rights organizations." These groups can operate legally, shielded by constitutional protections. Western authorities can't ban new groups without evidence of criminal activity, as targeting its ideology would be seen as infringing on religious freedom. Any effort to restrict such a group will result in accusations of "Islamophobia."

Unlike Muslim-majority countries, the West lacks the cultural and religious authority to draw a line between Islam's spiritual and political dimensions. It can only target specific groups, not the underlying ideas. Banning the Muslim Brotherhood in the West is like banning one brand of coffee while allowing others to sell the same blend under new labels. The ideology of political Islam, rooted in Islam's dual nature as both faith and governance, remains untouched. New groups will exploit Western freedoms, advancing the same goals through advocacy, education, and policy influence. When challenged, they can claim persecution, framing their critics as bigots.

This dynamic is impossible in Muslim-majority countries, where the state's Islamic credentials neutralize such defenses. The West's secular framework assumes religions are private matters of belief, not political systems. It fails to grasp that Islam, unlike other faiths, includes a blueprint for law, governance, and societal order. Muslim-majority governments, operating within Islam's ecosystem, can suppress this blueprint without undermining their legitimacy. The West, as an outsider, cannot.

To counter the spread of political Islam, the West must stop treating Islam solely as a religion. It needs to recognize Islam's legal code, governance model, and vision of supremacy as a political ideology. This would allow governments to regulate groups promoting sharia or Islamic rule without violating religious freedom, much like they regulate other political ideologies that threaten democratic values. Stripping Islam of its automatic religious protection in policy and law is the only way to address the ideology the Muslim Brotherhood represents.

ISRAEL AS A MODEL FOR MINORITY SURVIVAL IN THE ISLAMIC WORLD

Since the Islamic conquests of the Middle East in the 7th century, the region's diverse religious and ethnic minorities, Christians, Jews and others, have navigated a precarious existence under Islamic rule. The dhimmi system, which offered non-Muslims limited protections in exchange for taxes, legal and social subordination, entrenched a hierarchy that relegated minorities to perpetual inferiority. While this framework allowed for periods of relative tolerance, it also sowed the seeds of systemic discrimination, leaving minorities vulnerable to the shifting tides of political and religious fervor.

Among these minorities, the Jewish people faced a particularly harrowing journey, marked by centuries of persecution in both the Islamic world and Christian Europe. Yet, in 1948, the establishment of Israel transformed their narrative, creating a sovereign state where Jews could govern themselves, free from the yoke of external oppression. This achievement stands in stark contrast to the fate of Christian communities, who, despite their deep historical roots in the region, have faced a relentless decline under Islamic dominance. From the Copts of Egypt to the Assyrians of Iraq, Christians have endured systemic persecution, forced conversions, and displacement, often with the complicity of state authorities.

The Historical Decline of Minorities

To understand the imperative of Christian self-determination, one must first grapple with the historical trajectory of minorities in the Islamic world. The Islamic conquests of the 7th century reshaped the Middle East, transforming Christian and Jewish majorities into minorities under Islamic rule. The dhimmi system, while ostensibly protective, imposed heavy taxes, restricted religious expression, and prohibited non-Muslims from holding positions of authority. Over time, this system eroded the social, cultural, and political vitality of minority communities, setting the stage for their long-term decline.

For Jewish communities, life under Islamic rule was a complex interplay of tolerance and tribulation. In medieval Spain, the Granada massacre of 1066 saw Muslim mobs slaughter thousands of Jews, a grim reminder of their vulnerability. In Yemen, the Mawza Exile of 1679–1680 forced Jews into desolate regions, decimating their communities and livelihoods. Even in periods of relative prosperity, such as the cultural flourishing of Al-Andalus, Jews remained at the mercy of rulers whose benevolence could turn to brutality with a change in political winds. The Almohad dynasty's forced conversions in the 12th century and the periodic expulsions from North African cities underscored the precariousness of Jewish existence.

This pattern of persecution was not unique to the Islamic world. In Christian Europe, Jews faced similar horrors, from the massacres of the First Crusade to the Spanish Inquisition's relentless pursuit of "crypto-Jews" who had converted under duress. By the 19th century, the Enlightenment's promise of equality proved illusory, as the Dreyfus Affair in France and the pogroms in Russia exposed the depth of antisemitism even in "civilized" societies. These experiences convinced Jewish leaders like

Theodor Herzl that assimilation was a futile endeavor. Only a sovereign state could guarantee the safety and dignity of the Jewish people.

The Christian Decline

Christian communities, once the bedrock of the Middle East's cultural and religious landscape, have followed a similarly tragic path. In Egypt, the Copts, who predated Islam by centuries, comprised a significant portion of the population before the Arab conquest. Today, they constitute less than 10% of Egypt's population, their numbers diminished by centuries of discriminatory taxes, social exclusion, and periodic violence. The 2013 attacks on Coptic churches, following the ousting of Muslim Brotherhood leader Mohamed Morsi, saw dozens of churches burned and Christians killed, with little intervention from state authorities. These incidents reflect a broader pattern of state complicity or indifference, as Coptic girls are kidnapped and forcibly married to Muslims, and Christian communities face relentless pressure to conform or emigrate.

In Iraq, the Assyrian and Chaldean Christian populations have plummeted from 1.5 million in 2003 to fewer than 200,000 today, driven by sectarian violence and targeted persecution following the Iraqi war. The Islamic State's 2014 campaign in Mosul, marked by the infamous "Nun" symbol painted on Christian homes, forced thousands to flee, leaving behind centuries-old communities. In Syria, the civil war has reduced the Christian population from 1.5 million in 2011 to under 500,000, as extremist groups like ISIS and Jabhat al-Nusra have systematically targeted Christians for execution, enslavement, or displacement.

Lebanon, once a Christian-majority nation, offers a poignant case study in demographic and political decline. The Lebanese Civil War (1975–1990), coupled with Syrian occupation and the rise of Hezbollah, has eroded Christian influence, driving many to emigrate. Today, Christians make up less than a third of Lebanon's population, their political power curtailed by a confessional system that favors Muslim factions. Even in Jordan, often lauded for its tolerance, Christians face restrictions on religious expression, such as bans on public Christian symbols and prohibitions on converting Muslims. These examples illustrate a sobering truth: Christian communities, despite their historical rootedness, are dwindling under the weight of Islamic dominance.

The Failure of Assimilation

Like Jews in Europe, Christians in the Islamic world have pursued assimilation as a survival strategy, hoping to secure acceptance by adopting the cultural and religious norms of the majority. In Jordan, Christians often give their children Arabic names, participate in Islamic holidays like Ramadan, and avoid public displays of faith to deflect scrutiny. In Egypt, Coptic leaders have issued statements aligning with state narratives, condemning Israel or the West to avoid accusations of disloyalty. In Syria, churches have replaced references to "Israel" in Bible readings with euphemisms like "the ancient people" to appease authorities. These concessions, however, have not stemmed the tide of persecution but have instead eroded Christian identity and agency.

A chilling example of assimilation's failure occurred in Jordan in 2016, when a Christian journalist was assassinated for publishing a cartoon deemed offensive to Muslims, despite targeting ISIS. Rather than defending his freedom of expression, church leaders condemned him as a heretic, mimicking Islamic responses to dissent. This incident underscores the futility of appeasement: even when Christians align with the majority's values, they remain vulnerable to accusations of betrayal. Similarly, in the West Bank, churches have been burned by Islamic groups, and Christians in Bethlehem, once a Christian-majority city, now number fewer than 10,000, silenced and driven to emigrate.

These efforts to blend into Islamic society mirror the historical attempts of Jews to integrate into European culture. In the 18th century, Moses Mendelssohn advocated for Jews to adopt European languages and customs while maintaining their faith, believing this would lead to acceptance. Yet, the Dreyfus Affair and the Holocaust shattered this illusion, proving that assimilation could not shield Jews from hatred. For Christians in the Islamic world, the lesson is clear: no amount of cultural mimicry can guarantee safety in a region where their identity is inherently at odds with the dominant ideology.

The Power of Self-Determination

The establishment of Israel in 1948 marked a seismic shift in the Jewish narrative, transforming a persecuted minority into a sovereign nation capable of defending itself. Theodor Herzl, the architect of modern Zionism, was driven not by religious nostalgia but by an existential imperative. The Dreyfus Affair, which exposed the fragility of Jewish acceptance in "enlightened" France, and the pogroms in Russia, which killed thousands, convinced Herzl that assimilation was a dead end. His vision for a Jewish state was rooted in the recognition that only self-governance could ensure the survival of a people long targeted for their identity.

Israel's rejection of Islamic sovereignty was a radical act of defiance in a region where minorities were expected to submit. By creating a state where Jews could govern themselves, Israel established institutions that reflected their cultural, religious, and political values. Despite facing relentless hostility, wars in 1948, 1967, and 1973, and ongoing conflicts with neighboring states and non-state actors, Israel has thrived, building a robust economy, a formidable military, and a vibrant democracy. This success stands in stark contrast to the precarious existence of Christian minorities, who remain dependent on the goodwill of Islamic majorities or authoritarian regimes.

Israel's achievement is not merely a religious or cultural victory but a testament to the power of self-determination. The state's establishment in the shadow of the Holocaust, which claimed six million Jewish lives, underscores its existential necessity. For Jews, Israel is not just a homeland but a fortress, a place where they can live as equals rather than as tolerated guests. This model of sovereignty offers a profound lesson for Christians in the Islamic world, who face a similar existential threat.

The Case for Christian Self-Determination

The relentless decline of Christian communities in the Middle East demands a bold reimagining of their future. Living as second-class citizens under Islamic rule has proven unsustainable, as evidenced by the empty churches of Iraq, the burned sanctuaries of Egypt, the dead Christians in exploded churches in Syria, and the inability of the Christians in Lebanon to build a state. The temporary protections offered by authoritarian regimes, as in Jordan or Egypt, are fragile, collapsing in times of chaos or political upheaval. The rise of extremist groups, from the Muslim Brotherhood to ISIS, has only intensified the peril, leaving Christians with a stark choice: emigrate, assimilate, or fight for autonomy.

Israel's example points to the third path: self-determination. A sovereign Christian state, modeled on Israel's rejection of subjugation, would enable Christians to govern themselves, protect their cultural heritage, and ensure their security without the need to appease Muslim majorities. Lebanon, with its historical Christian majority and distinct regional identity, offers a viable starting point. The growing calls for federalism or partition in Lebanon reflect a recognition among Christians that autonomy is essential for survival. Mount Lebanon, with its Christian-majority population and historical significance, could serve as the territorial foundation for such a state.

This vision of Christian sovereignty need not be rooted in religious ideology, just as Israel's establishment was driven by existential necessity rather than solely religious narrative. A Christian state would prioritize practical goals: safeguarding human rights, preserving cultural identity, and providing a safe haven for a beleaguered minority. By establishing institutions that reflect their values, Christians could break free from the cycle of oppression and build a future where they are not merely tolerated but empowered.

Feasibility and Geopolitics

Critics may argue that Christian statehood is impractical, citing demographic fragmentation, geographic constraints, and the lack of a unified national identity. Unlike Jews, whose connection to the Land of Israel provided a clear territorial focus, Christians are dispersed across multiple countries and lack a single "holy land." However, Lebanon's Christian-majority regions offer a feasible territorial base, and the shared experience of persecution could forge a collective identity, much as the Holocaust galvanized Jewish nationalism. Moreover, the success of microstates like Qatar and Singapore demonstrates that size is not a barrier to sovereignty.

Another objection is that a Christian state would lack international support, given the geopolitical complexities of the Middle East. Israel's experience, however, shows that determined minority groups can secure allies through strategic diplomacy. Israel's alliances with the United States and, more recently, Gulf states like the UAE underscore the potential for a Christian state to navigate the region's power dynamics. While initial resistance from Islamic countries is likely, the growing recognition of minority rights on the global stage could bolster support for Christian self-determination.

Finally, some may argue that reforms within Islamic countries could protect Christians without the need for statehood. Yet, the historical record offers little hope for this approach. The protections afforded by regimes like Jordan's monarchy or Egypt's military are contingent on political stability, which is far from guaranteed. The rise of extremist movements, coupled with the failure of Arab states to uphold minority rights, suggests that reliance on external goodwill is a recipe for disaster. Israel's success demonstrates that only sovereignty can provide lasting security.

RADICAL IS THE NEW MIDDLE

My wife is probably the most balanced woman I know. She's a professional psychotherapist who began working at nineteen and never paused for a single day, until the birth of our child. From that moment on, she showed me what it means to be a woman in the most profound, life-giving way. She saturated our home with love, poured that love into our child every day, and embodied the role of mother without hesitation or complaint. Motherhood transformed her. It changed her sense of self, pulled her away from career dreams, and narrowed her social circle. It cost her something real. But in her own words, the cost was nothing compared to the joy of being there, present, attentive, engaged, every minute of every day for our child.

I tried to convince her to send him to daycare, just for a few hours a week, so she could have space to rest or reengage professionally. We even toured a few preschools. But she never went through with it. Her response was: "Going back to work and leaving him with someone else isn't a relief, it's the burden. Being with him is the gift." She also made sure I didn't feel forgotten. Even when I was drowning in the chaos of work, global events, and life transitions, she didn't demand more from me. She could have. Culturally, politically, she had every justification to hold me accountable or pull away. But instead, she covered for me when I was unavailable. She carried the weight without bitterness or resentment.

My wife is not a feminist, yet she is one of the most powerful women I know. If something were to happen to me, I have absolute confidence that she would rise to the occasion, taking the reins of our family with a competence that rivals any man's. She could provide, protect, lead; she possesses the skills, the intellect, the resilience to do everything traditionally ascribed to the male role. But she chooses not to. Not because she lacks the ability, but because she understands that blurring those roles doesn't liberate; it disrupts the delicate harmony that sustains a family. She lets the man fulfill his role as the pillar, the one who charts the course and shoulders the external storms, while she embodies the foundation upon which everything stands.

This isn't subjugation; it's synergy. She doesn't confuse the roles out of fear or tradition, but from a deep realization that a healthy family isn't an arena for competition, where husband and wife battle for dominance like gladiators in an endless fight. No, it's a partnership where each complements the other, their strengths interlocking like pieces of a divine puzzle. In this complementarity, there is no weakness, only amplified power, a union that weathers life's tempests with grace. Her choice is unapologetic, a bold stand against the tide that insists equality means sameness, proving instead that true equity flourishes in distinction.

My wife stands resolutely in the middle of the spectrum, that healthy, fertile ground where sanity prevails and extremes fade into irrelevance. She acknowledges, without hesitation or dilution, the historical truths that men, throughout the ages, have oppressed women, marginalizing them, denying them agency, and confining them to roles that stifled their potential. Yet, she also sees the danger in the pendulum's overcorrection, the radical feminist movements that propelled society from one end of the spectrum to the other, bypassing the balanced center entirely. What began as a necessary push for equality devolved into an erasure of distinctions, a war on the very roles that give life structure and meaning. This overcorrection hasn't freed women; it's isolated them further, confusing liberation with isolation from the complementary dynamics that enrich existence.

250 Broadway, New York

Feminism, born as a necessary revolt against genuine tyranny, has morphed into a radical doctrine that rejects biology, tradition, and complementarity. It views gender not as a natural duality but as a construct imposed by power structures, patriarchy, religion, colonialism. In this worldview, influenced by critical theory's binary lens of oppressor and oppressed, everything must be deconstructed. Men are perpetual villains, women eternal victims. Roles blur not for liberation but for destruction: the family unit, once a bastion of stability, is dismissed as a patriarchal invention; motherhood is reframed as a trap rather than a triumph.

This overcorrection stems from a deeper cultural plague: critical theory, which reduces the world to power dynamics. Pioneered by thinkers like Michel Foucault and Jacques Derrida, it posits that all meanings, gender, identity, truth, are socially constructed by the powerful to subjugate the weak. The "centers of power" include the male, the white, the Christian, the Jew, the capitalist, the Western nation, even God Himself. These must be dismantled for "liberation." Women must revolt against men; the colonized against the colonizer; the poor against the rich. Israel, as a symbol of Western success in a failed region, becomes the ultimate oppressor, while Palestinians are romanticized as pure victims.

The result is a snap from one tyranny to another. Where once women were marginalized, now men suffocate under MeToo's blanket accusations, forced to atone for ancestral sins. White individuals must bear perpetual guilt, silenced in discussions of race. Western nations, despite their innovations in democracy, science, and human rights, are branded eternal colonialists. Success itself becomes suspect: the powerful are always wrong, the weak always right. Truth dissolves into relativism; identity fragments into 200 genders, leaving generations adrift in confusion.

This culture, obsessed with dismantling every structure built by traditional power, has found in Islam a convenient ally. Islam's civilizational stagnation, caused by its own theological rigidity, has left it defeated, and being non-Western, and "brown", defeated by the West, made it a combination that, in the eyes of the radical left, as the ultimate oppressed victim. As a result, Islam is enlisted as a comrade in the crusade against the true centers of power.

In this narrative, Israel stands as everything Islam is not, successful, resilient, a flourishing outpost of modernity amid chaos. For that very reason, it is vilified, as a symbol of whiteness, Western imperialism, Judeo-Christian dominance, and colonial entitlement. In this distorted moral framework, Israel becomes the archetypal villain, a stand-in for all that must be obliterated in the name of "justice."

This is the poisonous worldview nurtured in the home of Mahmood Mamdani, the father of Zohran Mamdani the mayoral candidate in NYC. It is a philosophy that casts America as the "Great Satan," and attributes Islamic terrorism not to the Islamic theology or supremacist doctrines, but to the American imperialistic policies. It reframes 9/11 as a predictable response to imperial overreach. Suicide bombings are reframed as political statements, stripped of their theological motivations, and even rape is perversely rationalized as a tool of anti-colonial resistance. At its core, this ideology envisions a "globalized intifada", a worldwide violent uprising where the oppressed are glorified for annihilating their oppressors. This is why the activists cheer for Hamas, because Hamas does what they fantasize about.

This is the same ideological virus that fuels calls to defund the police because they are seen as foot soldiers of the oppressor class. In this worldview, law enforcement is not a mechanism of order, but a weapon wielded by white, Western, male, capitalist power to maintain its grip on society. The nation-state itself is reframed as a colonial construct, a geographic lie imposed by imperial powers to enshrine privilege and restrict the movement of the oppressed. Borders, like gender or truth, are to be deconstructed. Laws are violence. Sovereignty is oppression. And anyone who defends these structures is labeled a fascist, a reactionary, a defender of the "old world" they are determined to burn to the ground.

If Zohran Mamdani enters the New York City Hall at 250 Broadway, it will be the institutionalization of an ideology that sees American power as inherently evil, Western civilization as a colonial crime, and Judeo-Christian values as systems of oppression to be dismantled. Mamdani inherits a worldview rooted in the radical rejection of the very foundations that built New York into the capital of modernity. His rise to power would mark the mainstreaming of a philosophy that dreams of tearing down law enforcement, diluting national identity, and absolving jihadist terror under the guise of resistance. Public schools will be hijacked to indoctrinate children into viewing themselves through the lens of victimhood and grievance. capitalism will be portrayed as theft. Under Mamdani's ideological regime, justice will be inverted, where success is a mark of guilt, and criminality a badge of resistance.

The Case for The Middle

The middle is where clarity lives. It is where truth is not bent to fit narratives or manipulated to preserve comfort. It doesn't flinch under the weight of political correctness or ideological pressure. It doesn't care who's offended. What critical theory poisons, the middle restores. Where it sees oppression in design, the middle sees order. Where it cries for deconstruction, the middle builds. Where it brands all strength as abuse, the middle distinguishes between tyranny and responsibility. And where it tears down the very concept of truth, the middle insists: truth is not a construct. It is not whiteness. It is not colonialism. It is not Christian supremacy. It is what it is, unbending, clear, uncomfortable, but necessary for civilization to stand.

This is the posture my wife embodies. She chose a life too much of the world no longer honors, and in doing so, she exposed the bankruptcy of an ideology that calls motherhood slavery and femininity weakness. Her clarity is revolutionary. And so is mine. Because I, too, stand in the middle. And that is why I expose the threat of Islam. Both ends of the spectrum have abandoned that clarity. The radical left has collapsed into a worldview that filters everything through power and victimhood, making Islam untouchable because of its position in the narrative hierarchy. Meanwhile, the fearful right attempts to sidestep confrontation by isolating "Islamism" as the problem, preserving the illusion that Islam itself is benign. Both responses are dishonest, and dangerous.

The middle does not submit to either. The middle does not care for appeasement or overcorrection. The middle reads the Qur'an *and* the hadiths. It understands the concept of *dar al-Islam* and *dar al-harb*.* It knows that Muhammad was not just a prophet but a warlord, that Sharia is not a spiritual guide but a total system of governance. The middle sees clearly that the threat is not a few extremists but the theological machinery that produces them, generation after generation. And it dares to say so.

---

* Dar al-Islam ("the abode of Islam") and Dar al-Harb ("the abode of war") are classical Islamic jurisprudential categories dividing the world into two spheres: territories under Islamic rule versus territories outside Islamic control.

Exposing the truth about Islam is not bigotry. It is not "Islamophobia." It is intellectual integrity. And only from the middle can such integrity be practiced, because only the middle is free from ideological captivity. It has no need to protect Islam to prove it's tolerant. It has no need to demonize Muslims to feel superior. It simply tells the truth and prepares accordingly.

This is the same middle that sees the threat of Zohran Mamdani. A man raised on grievance theory, schooled in critical ideology, and formed within a religious tradition that has historically fused theology with political power. He now stands on the doorstep of institutional influence in the capital of the modern world. Mamdani is the embodiment of both distortions, and his rise is the natural result of a culture that rewards grievance and punishes clarity. His success would not just mark a shift in political priorities, it would represent the normalization of an ideology that undermines the very structures that made a city like New York possible in the first place.

This is why the middle matters now more than ever. Not the shallow center that tries to please everyone. Not the neutral zone that avoids hard questions. But the clear-headed, fact-based, truth-telling middle, where ideas are tested, not protected. Where doctrine is examined. Where ideologies are not judged by their intentions, but by their outcomes. Where Islam is neither protected from scrutiny nor distorted by ignorance. Where civilization is not something to apologize for, but something to defend.

NOTES

INTRODUCTION

1. Hamas's October 7, 2023 attack killed over 1,200 people, mostly civilians, and took more than 200 hostages (*BBC News*, Oct. 8, 2023; *New York Times*, Oct. 8, 2023).
2. Dec. 31, 2023, reported approximately 15,000 demonstrators at the New Year's Eve pro-Palestinian march in downtown Chicago. https://titan-security.com/chicago-events-and-demonstrations-december-15-to-december-31-2023/
3. Between Oct. 7 and May 12, the U.S. recorded about 3,700 demonstration events tied to the Israel-Palestine conflict, including ~1,150 encampments at nearly 150 colleges (Princeton Bridging Divides Initiative, May 2024).
4. Paul Kessler, 69, died of blunt-force trauma after being struck with a megaphone during a pro-Palestinian rally in Thousand Oaks, California, on Nov. 5, 2023. A suspect was later charged with involuntary manslaughter https://abcnews.go.com/US/demonstrator-stand-trial-death-jewish-man-november-israel/story?id=110286757
5. On May 21, 2025, Israeli Embassy staffers Yaron Lischinsky and Sarah Lynn Milgrim were fatally shot outside the Capital Jewish Museum in Washington, D.C., after attending a diplomatic event. The suspect, Elias Rodriguez, was arrested at the scene while reportedly shouting "Free, free Palestine" https://www.cnn.com/2025/05/22/us/lischinsky-milgrim-israel-embassy-shooting
6. @ShabbosK, X, July 11, 2024, https://x.com/ShabbosK/status/1811234567890123456.
7. Estimates place the Syrian war death toll between 580,000 (May 2021) and over 656,000 (March 2025). (Syrian Observatory for Human Rights; *New York Post*, Dec. 17, 2024).
8. UNICEF and AP report that more than 17 million Yemenis face hunger, including over 1 million children under five suffering acute malnutrition (*AP News*, July 2023; UNICEF USA, 2023).
9. Over 7,000 Christians were killed in Nigeria in the first 220 days of 2025, with 7,800 abducted. Intersociety reports total Christian casualties since 2009 at approximately 125,000 (*Christian Post*, Aug. 2025; *Catholic World Report*, Aug. 12, 2025).

10. Student-led activism for Palestinian rights has surged in Western universities, with groups like Students for Justice in Palestine (SJP) organizing protests and pushing for divestment from companies tied to Israeli policies. Green, E. (2023, December 15). How a Student Group Is Politicizing a Generation on Palestine. *The New Yorker*. https://www.newyorker.com/news/annals-of-education/how-a-generation-is-being-politicized-on-palestine
11. As of 2023, UNRWA registered approximately 489,000 Palestinian refugees in Lebanon, who face legal restrictions prohibiting property ownership, requiring difficult-to-obtain work permits, barring them from 39 professions. U.S. Department of State. (2024). 2023 Country Reports on Human Rights Practices: Lebanon. https://www.state.gov/reports/2023-country-reports-on-human-rights-practices/lebanon/
12. Prior to the Syrian civil war, over 560,000 Palestinian refugees were registered in Syria, facing discrimination and surveillance. Szydzisz, M. (2018). Palestinian Refugees in Syria During the Syrian Civil War. TEKA of Political Science and International Relations. https://journals.umcs.pl/teka/article/view/7849
13. Palestinian Refugees of Egypt: What Exit Options Are Left for Them? Refuge: Canada's Journal on Refugees. https://refuge.journals.yorku.ca/index.php/refuge/article/view/21329 (for Egypt); Amnesty International. (2007). Iraq: Human rights abuses against Palestinian refugees. https://www.amnesty.org/en/documents/mde14/030/2007/en/ (for Iraq)
14. Operation Summer Rains was an Israeli military operation in the Gaza Strip launched in June 2006 following the capture of IDF soldier Gilad Shalit. Wikipedia. (2023). Gilad Shalit. https://en.wikipedia.org/wiki/Gilad_Shalit
15. Black September refers to the 1970 conflict in Jordan. Wikipedia. (2023). Black September. https://en.wikipedia.org/wiki/Black_September
16. Jyllands-Posten Muhammad cartoons controversy. https://en.wikipedia.org/wiki/Jyllands-Posten_Muhammad_cartoons_controversy
17. Sheikh Khalid Al-Rashid's sermon O' Ummah Of Muhammad. https://www.youtube.com/watch?v=POL8CLBaBNU
18. The Systemic Elimination of Critics in Islam. https://rrimedia.org/Worldviews/Islam/Studies-in-Islam/ArtMID/1464/ArticleID/100/The-Systemic-Elimination-of-Critics-in-Islam
19. Khaybar, Khaybar, oh Jews, the Army of Mohammed will return. https://www.adl.org/resources/backgrounder/chant-khaybar-khaybar-oh-jews-army-mohammed-will-return

20. The president of Egypt is assassinated, https://www.history.com/this-day-in-history/october-6/the-president-of-egypt-is-assassinated
21. Introducing Marxism: Understanding Israel-Palestine. *Socialism Today*. https://socialismtoday.org/introducing-marxism-understanding-israel-palestine
22. Islamist terrorist attacks in the world 1979-2024 https://www.fondapol.org/en/study/islamist-terrorist-attacks-in-the-world-1979-2024/

1. WHAT IS ISLAM?

1. Nicole Brisch, "Religion and Power: Divine Kingship in the Ancient World and Beyond," Institute for the Study of Ancient Cultures (University of Chicago, 2011), https://isac.uchicago.edu/research/symposia/religion-and-power-divine-kingship-ancient-world-and-beyond-0.
2. "Pharaoh: Born of the Gods – E5," National Gallery of Victoria, https://www.ngv.vic.gov.au/labels/pharaoh-born-of-the-gods/.
3. Beau Branson et al., "The Intertwining of Philosophy and Religion in the Western Tradition," in Introduction to Philosophy: Philosophy of Religion (Rebus Community, 2020), https://press.rebus.community/intro-to-phil-of-religion/chapter/the-intertwining-of-philosophy-and-religion-in-the-western-tradition-2/.
4. Jan Garrett, "Homer's Gods, Plato's Gods," Western Kentucky University, https://people.wku.edu/jan.garrett/pgods.htm.
5. Early Roman law clearly intertwined with religious ritual. For instance, the *ius civile*—law applying to Roman citizens—was deeply bound to religion. Its rituals and formalism (e.g., *mancipatio*, a formal property transfer) trace back to Etruscan, ritualistic origins.
6. Judaism On The Worth Of Every Person," Jewish Virtual Library, https://www.jewishvirtuallibrary.org/judaism-on-the-worth-of-every-person.
7. Revolution in Wittenberg, https://www.britannica.com/biography/Martin-Luther/Diet-of-Worms?utm_source=chatgpt.com
8. "Did America Have a Christian Founding?," The Heritage Foundation, June 7, 2011, https://www.heritage.org/political-process/report/did-america-have-christian-founding.
9. "Arabian religion," Britannica, https://www.britannica.com/topic/Arabian-religion.
10. "The Goddesses of Pre-Islamic Arabia (Al-Lāt, Al-'Uzzā, Manāt)," Academia.edu, https://www.academia.edu/24737662/The_Goddess

es_of_Pre_Islamic_Arabia_Al_L%C4%81t_Al_Uzz%C4%81_Man%C4%81t_.
11. The pagan origin of the word, "Allah". https://www.bible.ca/islam/islam-allah-pre-islamic-origin.htm
12. "JUDAISM IN PRE-ISLAMIC ARABIA," Cambridge Core, https://resolve.cambridge.org/core/services/aop-cambridge-core/content/view/C9F5F6DD0AF09B26594CD08D742C7A4F/9780521517171c9_294-331.pdf/judaism-in-pre-islamic-arabia.pdf.
13. "The History and Significance of the Meccan Hajj: from Pre-Islam to the Present," Leiden University Scholarly Publications, https://scholarlypublications.universiteitleiden.nl/access/item%253A3663459/view.
14. *"Al-gharānīq al-'ulā"* Sūrat al-Najm 53:19–20. Ibn Ishaq, *Sīrat Rasūl Allāh*. al-Tabari, *Tārīkh al-Rusul wa'l-Mulūk* (vol. VI, pp. 107–112); and cited via al-Waqidi. Related narrations on the mass prostration appear in Sahih Bukhari (Vol. 2, Book 19, Hadith 176–177; Vol. 6, Book 60, Hadith 385).
15. "Kulayb b. Rabīʿa," Encyclopaedia of Islam Online, https://referenceworks.brillonline.com/entries/encyclopaedia-of-islam-2/kulayb-b-rabia-SIM_4563.
16. "Abū Ṭālib," Encyclopaedia of Islam Online, https://referenceworks.brillonline.com/entries/encyclopaedia-of-islam-2/abu-talib-SIM_0240.
17. "The Constitution of Medina," Oxford Bibliographies, https://www.oxfordbibliographies.com/display/document/obo-9780195390155/obo-9780195390155-0034.xml.
18. "Qiblah - Islamic Direction, Prayer, Kaaba," Britannica, https://www.britannica.com/topic/qiblah.
19. "Sunnah | Definition, Significance, & Examples," Britannica, https://www.britannica.com/topic/Sunnah.
20. "The difference between the Meccan and Medinan surahs in Quran,"https://www.meforum.org/the-qurans-turn-to-violence
21. Luther and the Jews: A Record of Oppression and Hatred," Lutheran Church–Missouri Synod, https://www.lcms.org/about/beliefs/luther-and-jews.
22. Uri Rubin, *The Assassination of Kaʿb b. al-Ashraf*, Oriens 32 [1990], pp. 65–71
23. "Antoine-Louis-Claude, Comte Destutt de Tracy," Britannica, https://www.britannica.com/biography/Antoine-Louis-Claude-Comte-Destutt-de-Tracy.
24. The Definition of a political ideology, Stanford Encyclopedia of Philosophy. https://plato.stanford.edu/entries/ideology/

25. Andrew Heywood, *Politics*, 4th ed. (Basingstoke: Palgrave Macmillan, 2013), 28–29, "Concept: Ideology." Defines ideology as "a more or less coherent set of ideas that provides a basis for organized political action," and specifies three features (diagnosis of the present order, a desired future, and a route to change).
26. Dar al-Islam / dar al-harb, https://www.brown.edu/Departments/Joukowsky_Institute/courses/islamiccivilizations/7968.html
27. In his commentary on Quran 9:29, al-Qurtubi (d. 1273 CE, a prominent Maliki scholar) emphasizes the broad, unqualified scope of the command to fight, https://www.altafsir.com/Tafasir.asp?tMadhNo=1&tTafsirNo=5&tSoraNo=9&tAyahNo=29&tDisplay=yes&UserProfile=0&LanguageId=1
28. Sex, Wine, and Animals: The Caprices of the Caliphs, https://raseef22.net/english/article/1066865-caliphs-and-their-caprices
29. Religion and The State in Ibn Khaldun's Muqaddimah, https://www.academia.edu/7563563/Religion_and_The_State_in_Ibn_Khalduns_Muqaddimah
30. The Turkish republic of Kemal Atatürk, https://www.britannica.com/biography/Kemal-Ataturk/The-Turkish-republic

2. THE ISLAMIC WAR ON ISRAEL

1. The Ottoman Empire was the foremost and longest-lived of the Islamic empires of the early modern world. https://openstax.org/books/world-history-volume-2/pages/4-2-the-ottoman-empire.
2. "The Ottoman empire's secular history undermines sharia claims,"https://www.theguardian.com/commentisfree/belief/2011/oct/07/ottoman-empire-secular-history-sharia.
3. Sharif Hussein and the campaign for a modern Arab empire, https://aeon.co/essays/sharif-hussein-and-the-campaign-for-a-modern-arab-empire.
4. See, Hussein-McMahon correspondence, https://www.britannica.com/topic/Husayn-McMahon-correspondence
5. Correspondence between Sir Henry McMahon, G.C.M.G., His Majesty's High Commissioner at Cairo and the Sherif Hussein of Mecca, July 1915-March 1916," Archive.org, https://archive.org/details/mcmahon5957.
6. The Papers of Al-Sharif Hussein Bin Ali," aalalbayt.org, https://www.aalalbayt.org/wp-content/uploads/2020/11/The-Papers-of-al-Sharif-Hussein-bin-Ali-ebook.pdf.
7. "Jihad and Islam in World War I," Leiden University Press, 2016, https://dokumen.pub/jihad-and-islam-in-world-war-i-studies-on-

the-ottoman-jihad-at-the-centenary-of-snouck-hurgronjes-holy-war-made-in-germany-9789400602335.html.
8. Alan Dowty, "Arabs and Jews in Ottoman Palestine," Indiana University Press, 2019, https://www.rahs-open-lid.com/wp-content/uploads/2024/01/Dowty-Alan-Arabs-and-Jews-in-Ottoman-Palestine_-Two-Worlds-Collide-Indiana-University-Press-2019.pdf.
9. "The Land Question in Palestine, 1917-1939," University of North Carolina Press, https://uncpress.org/book/9780807841785/the-land-question-in-palestine-1917-1939/.
10. The First Aliyah," Jewish Virtual Library, https://www.jewishvirtuallibrary.org/the-first-aliyah.
11. "To the People and Residents across the Jordan," *Barid al-Yawm* [*Daily Mail*] (Jerusalem), 20 July 1920, p. 2, Jrayed—Arabic Newspaper Archive, National Library of Israel. https://jrayed.org/en/newspapers/baridalyaum/1920/07/20/01/article/3?utm_source=chatgpt.com
12. "Herzliya Hebrew Gymnasium," Jewish Virtual Library, https://www.jewishvirtuallibrary.org/herzliya-hebrew-gymnasium.
13. "Arab Immigration to Historic Palestine: A Survey," CAMERA, May 1, 2001, https://www.camera.org/article/arab-immigration-to-historic-palestine-a-survey/.
14. "Peel Commission Report (1937)," Jewish Virtual Library, https://www.jewishvirtuallibrary.org/the-peel-commission-report-july-1937.
15. "Hope Simpson Report (1930)," Jewish Virtual Library, https://www.jewishvirtuallibrary.org/hope-simpson-report.
16. Alan Dowty, "Arabs and Jews in Ottoman Palestine," Indiana University Press, 2019, https://iupress.org/9780253038654/arabs-and-jews-in-ottoman-palestine/.
17. Period 7-1-1: Britain's Promises to Arabs and Jews," Boston University, https://www.bu.edu/mzank/Jerusalem/p/period7-1-1.htm.
18. 400 years of Ottoman rule in Lebanon, https://www.dailysabah.com/op-ed/2019/09/12/400-years-of-ottoman-rule-in-lebanon-an-uneasy-negotiation
19. [1] "Sunnis in Beirut pledged allegiance to Sharif Hussein," *The Modern History of Lebanon*, Kamal S. Salibi, 1965, p. 161.
20. Muslims' dissatisfaction with the creation of Greater Lebanon is well-documented. Source: https://www.jstor.org/stable/4283175, p.41
21. A country with an Arab face and a Christian heart, https://www.omnesmag.com/en/news/the-mosaic-liban/
22. The Divisive Drafting of the 1926 Lebanese Constitution," Cambridge University Press, https://www.cambridge.org/core/books/constitution-writing-religion-and-democracy/secularism-in-a-sectarian-soci

ety-the-divisive-drafting-of-the-1926-lebanese-constitution/
67C84DB62FAC383536F395D7B2FC74BA.
23. "Nasserism in Lebanon," Academia.edu, https://www.academia.edu/220194/Nasserism_in_Lebanon.
24. "The Palestinian Factor in the Lebanese Civil War," Middle East Journal, https://www.jstor.org/stable/4325558.
25. "Hezbollah's 1985 Manifesto," Wilson Center, https://www.wilsoncenter.org/publication/hezbollahs-1985-manifesto.
26. MEMRI TV Archival Clip Hassan Nasrallah Laying Out," MEMRI, https://www.memri.org/reports/leading-saudi-daily-al-arabiyanet-shows-memri-tv-archival-clip-hassan-nasrallah-laying-out.
27. "The Taif Agreement," Conciliation Resources, https://www.c-r.org/accord/lebanon/taif-agreement.
28. "Why Lebanon Was Once Called the Switzerland of the Middle East," The Collector, https://www.thecollector.com/lebanon-switzerland-middle-east/.
29. "The Syrian Muslim Brotherhood and Violence," Cambridge University Press, https://www.cambridge.org/core/books/muslim-brotherhood-in-syria/syrian-muslim-brotherhood-and-violence/0416C178429F56FACB99D7A841AF624A.
30. Following the Bar Kokhba revolt, the Roman Empire renamed the province of Judaea, www.britannica.com/place/Palestine/Roman-Palestine
31. The area later known as Mandatory Palestine was split into the sanjaks of Jerusalem, Nablus and Acre, www.palquest.org/en/highlight/155/ottoman-territorial-reorganization-1840-1917
32. The Jewish Agency, initially called the Jewish Agency for Palestine, www.israelforever.org/state/Mandate_for_Palestine_Jewish_State
33. See, https://www.crwflags.com/fotw/flags/xo-auji.html
34. From 1948 to the early 1970s, over 850,000 Jews were displaced from Arab countries, www.gov.il/en/pages/jewish-refugees-expelled-from-arab-lands-and-from-iran-30-november-2017
35. In 1955, Egyptian leader Gamal Abdel Nasser contacted Quaker relief workers to explore the possibility of mediated peace talks with Israel, www.pym.org/middle-east-collaborative/1955-2
36. In the aftermath of the Six-Day War, Saudi Arabia provided substantial financial support to Egypt, and one of the political conditions was the release of Muslim Brotherhood prisoners, www.britannica.com/topic/Muslim-Brotherhood
37. Abd al-Malik built the Dome of the Rock in 691 CE to redirect Muslim pilgrimage and anchor *al-Masjid al-Aqṣā* to Jerusalem. www.sixdaywar.org/jerusalem/jerusalem-in-muslim-tradition

38. Israel's Declaration of Independence www.jewishvirtuallibrary.org/the-declaration-of-the-establishment-of-the-state-of-israel
39. Khaled al-Azm bluntly admitted: *"Since 1948, it is we who made them leave ... Then we exploited them ... in the service of political purposes."* www.cojs.org/1948-palestinian-refugees-khaled-al-azm
40. Egypt administered the Gaza Strip, while Jordan controlled and annexed the West Bank, www.britannica.com/place/West-Bank
41. Mahmoud al-Zahar: Palestine is not our project, https://youtu.be/VBAMMykiOuE?si=y4kRP1Yfnr-UkJXD
42. The 1988 Hamas Charter explicitly identifies the organization as "one of the branches of the Muslim Brotherhood in Palestine." www.govinfo.gov/content/pkg/CHRG-115hhrg31367/html/CHRG-115hhrg31367.htm
43. Al-Azhar expressed pride in Hamas's October 7 actions, saying the Palestinian resistance "breathed spirit and faith into us." www.inss.org.il/publication/al-azhar/
44. the Banu Qurayza were executed, while women and children were enslaved. www.britannica.com/topic/Siege-of-Banu-Qurayza
45. Prophet Muhammad is recorded as saying: "I will certainly expel the Jews and the Christians from Arabia and I shall leave only Muslims in it." www.sunnah.com/abudawud/20/3030
46. Hadith recorded in *Sahih Muslim*, prohibiting greeting Jews and Christians first and commanding to "force them to the narrowest part of the road." www.sunnah.com/muslim:2167
47. Prophet Muhammad told all—but ʿAlī lay in his bed, risking his life so the pursuers would be misled. www.tohed.com/threads/migration-to-medina-and-hazrat-alis-sleep-on-the-prophets-bed.728
48. • Between **2000 and 2010**, **1,194 Israelis and foreigners** were killed, www.govinfo.gov/content/pkg/CHRG-115hhrg31367/html/CHRG-115hhrg31367.htm

3. WHY ISLAM IS INCOMPATIBLE WITH THE WEST

1. Tom Holland: www.littlebrown.co.uk/little-brown-news/2023/05/04/read-an-excerpt-from-dominion-by-tom-holland?utm_source=chatgpt.com
2. See, www.un.org/development/desa/pd/sites/www.un.org.development.desa.pd/files/undesa_pd_2025_intlmigstock_2024_key_facts_and_figures_advance-unedited.pdf
3. Richard Dawkins' interview. www.ncregister.com/cna/famous-atheist-richard-dawkins-says-he-considers-himself-a-cultural-christian

4. @holland_tom, X, https://x.com/holland_tom/status/1774680923113398287
5. Friedrich Nietzsche observed that once the Christian faith is abandoned, "Christian morality" collapses with it: *Twilight of the Idols* (1889). www.gutenberg.org/files/52263/52263-h/52263-h.htm
6. Samuel Huntington warned that "conflicts between civilizations are the greatest conflicts, *The Clash of Civilizations and the Remaking of World Order* (1996). www.simonandschuster.com/books/The-Clash-of-Civilizations-and-the-Remaking-of-World-Order/Samuel-P-Huntington/9781451628975
7. Germany spent over €1.4 billion on integration courses from 2005–2013 and about €2.1 billion in 2016, yet only ~57 percent passed the B1 German test by 2012. www.bamf.de/Integration-Kurse-Ausgaben
8. See, https://youtu.be/muN4NCshbsA?si=Y3JLL2mc72v4vuR8
9. Over the past decades, jihadist groups carried out more than 60,000 terrorist attacks worldwide. (www.fondapol.org/en/study/islamist-terrorist-attacks-in-the-world-1979-2024
10. In Ibn Ishaq's account, after killing Asma bint Marwan, Muhammad assured Umayr: "Two goats will not butt their heads about her." www.answering-islam.org/Silas/asma.htm
11. Abu Ubaydah killed his own father at Badr, affirming faith over kinship, and Quran 58:22 was revealed in that context. www.alislam.org/articles/abu-ubaidah-bin-jarrah/
12. See, Al-Targhib (enticement) and al-Tarhib (threat) are used in Islamic education as complementary tools to motivate moral conduct. www.aensiweb.com/old/jasr/jasr/2012/3249-3252.pdf
13. Kohlberg's theory identifies six stages of moral reasoning, from obedience to universal principles. www.simplypsychology.org/kohlberg.html
14. See, Camerer's 1997 study of NYC taxi drivers showed they stopped once they hit a daily target, even if demand was high. www.nber.org/papers/w4948
15. Kahneman and Tversky's prospect theory (1979) introduced *loss aversion*: losses loom larger than gains. www.jstor.org/stable/1914185
16. See, www.soundvision.com/article/the-moakha-system-how-the-prophet-joined-diverse-muslims-hearts
17. www.wikiislam.net/wiki/Muhammad's_Marriages
18. "Hasan, often married four wives in one sitting and then divorced four wives in one sitting." www.al-islam.org/serat-vol-4-no-3-1978-imam-hasan-myth-his-divorces
19. Muhammad gave Safiyya to himself by instructing Dihya to take any

other captive; some narrations say Dihya received seven other slaves in return. www.wikiislam.net/wiki/Safiyah_bint_Huyayy

20. *Sahih Muslim* 1403a: "A woman advances and retreats like Satan… so when one of you sees a woman, let him go to his wife." www.sunnah.com/muslim/20/1403a

21. After seeing a woman, Muhammad went to his wife, Zainab, to relieve his desire and later instructed his companions that when struck by carnal thoughts, they too should "go to their wife," as recorded in *Sahih Muslim* 1403a. www.sunnah.com/muslim/20/1403a

4. REBRANDING ISLAM

1. See, John Rawls (*Political Liberalism*, 1993). www.hup.harvard.edu/catalog.php?isbn=9780231130899
2. Rawls contrasted an "overlapping consensus" with a mere *modus vivendi*— (*Political Liberalism*, 1993). www.hup.harvard.edu/catalog.php?isbn=9780231130899
3. Dr. Peter Hammond, *Slavery, Terrorism and Islam: The Historical Roots and Contemporary Threat* (Christian Liberty Books, 2005). www.frontline.org.za
4. Sweden's Muslim population, https://www.pewresearch.org/religion/2017/11/29/europes-growing-muslim-population/
5. Germany's Muslim population grew from approximately 3.7% (around 3 million) in 2005 to around 6.6% (5.5 million) by 2023. www.deutsche-islam-konferenz.de/EN/DatenFakten/daten-fakten_node.html
6. The UK's Muslim population, www.ons.gov.uk/peoplepopulationandcommunity/culturalidentity/religion/articles/religioninenglandandwales2011/2012-12-11
7. See, www.meforum.org/middle-east-quarterly/coming-to-terms-fundamentalists-or-islamists
8. *See*, www.gov.uk/government/publications/prevent-duty-guidance
9. Edward Said's *Orientalism* (1978) www.cambridge.org/core/books/orientalism/EDWARD-SAID-1978
10. See, www.arabworldbooks.com/en/e-zine/karen-armstrong-on-islam
11. Ibn Taymiyya explicitly rejected it, saying: *"There is no known basis for this hadith, and it is not a saying of the Prophet"* (Majmū' al-Fatāwā, vol. 11, p. 197).
12. David Horowitz's book *Unholy Alliance: Radical Islam and the American Left* (2004, Regnery Publishing)

13. https://www.memri.org/reports/saudi-government-paper-billions-spent-saudi-royal-family-spread-islam-every-corner-earth
14. External funding of radical mosques in Europe https://www.europarl.europa.eu/doceo/document/E-9-2022-000345_EN.html
15. How Middle Eastern States Leverage Mosques to Influence Western Muslim Communities https://www.meforum.org/mef-observer/how-middle-eastern-states-leverage-mosques-to-influence-western-muslim-communities
16. https://www.ncr-iran.org/en/news/terrorism-a-fundamentalism/iran-news-germanys-bavaria-exposes-tehrans-terror-network-bans-islamic-center-hamburg/

5. THE FOREIGN GOD

1. See, https://encyclopedia.ushmm.org/content/en/article/lebensraum
2. See, www.ndl.go.jp/constitution/e/shiryo/03/056shoshi.html
3. @MarinaMedvin, X, https://x.com/MarinaMedvin/status/1958496032821592374
4. six of the top eight countries searching for pornography are Muslim-majority,www.business-standard.com/article/news-ani/pak-occupies-top-slot-in-google-s-list-of-most-porn-searching-countries-115011900366_1.html

6. THE NEW FRONTIERS

1. Gallup: https://news.gallup.com/topic/palestinian-territory.aspx
2. Pew Research Center (via Jewish Virtual Library): https://www.jewishvirtuallibrary.org/american-public-opinion-toward-israel-an-overview

ABOUT THE AUTHOR

Danny Burmawi is an author, political commentator, and founder of the Ideological Defense Institute. Born in Jordan in 1988, he converted from Islam to Christianity as a young man—a decision that forced him to leave his homeland and shaped the course of his life's work. At nineteen, he moved to Lebanon, where he spent fourteen years immersed in the region's political and religious complexities. During that time, he founded and led multiple nonprofit organizations serving across the Middle East.

Danny holds a Master's degree in Theological Studies, and *Islam, Israel and the West* is his third published book. He now resides in the United States with his wife and son, where he continues his mission of educating the Western public and policymakers about the threat of Islamism and other tyrannical ideologies.

www.ingramcontent.com/pod-product-compliance
Lightning Source LLC
Chambersburg PA
CBHW020536030426
42337CB00013B/872